NATIONAL GEOGRAPHIC | STUDENT'S BOOK **3**

SERIES
JoAnn (Jodi) Crandall
Joan Kang Shin

AUTHOR
Rob Sved

NATIONAL GEOGRAPHIC LEARNING | **CENGAGE Learning**

Australia • Brazil • Japan • Korea • Mexico • Singapore • Spain • United Kingdom • United States

Unit 0

Welcome to Our Class

1 Look, listen and say. TR: A2

How do you say *borrador* in English?

It's a *rubber.*

How do you spell *scissors?*

s-c-i-s-s-o-r-s

Could you repeat that, please?

Of course, s-c-i-s-s-o-r-s.

I don't understand. Can you help me, please?

Yes, of course.

What's the difference between *next to* and *in front of?*

I can show you.

Seasons and months

2 **Look and listen.** TR: A3

spring

summer

autumn

winter

3 **Listen, point and say.** TR: A4

4 **Look, listen and say.** TR: A5

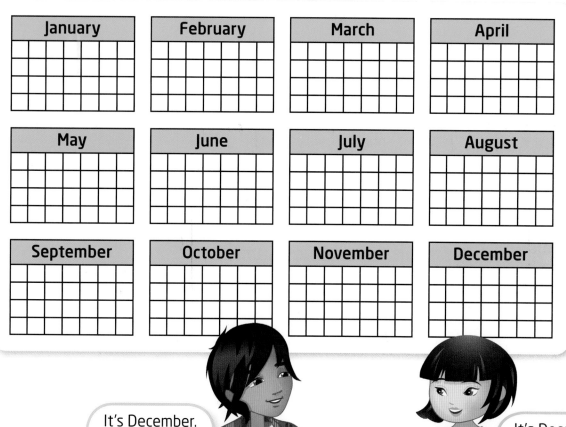

| January | February | March | April |

| May | June | July | August |

| September | October | November | December |

It's December.
It's cold here.

It's December,
but it's hot here.

5 **Look, listen and say.** TR: A6

20	21	22	23	24
twenty	twenty-one	twenty-two	twenty-three	twenty-four

25	26	27	28	29
twenty-five	twenty-six	twenty-seven	twenty-eight	twenty-nine

30	40	50	60	70
thirty	forty	fifty	sixty	seventy

80	90	100	101	102
eighty	ninety	one hundred	one hundred and one	one hundred and two

200

two hundred

1,000	1,000,000	1,000,000,000
one thousand	one million	one billion

+	–	=
plus	minus	equals

6 **Work with a friend.** Listen. Do the maths together. Listen to check your answers. TR: A7

24 + 2 =	80 + 9 =	300 – 50 =
100 + 10 =	35 + 5 =	1,000 + 1,000 =
60 + 20 =	40 – 30 =	99 – 9 =

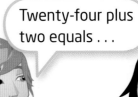

Twenty-four plus two equals . . .

Twenty-six!

7 Look, listen and say. TR: A8

1st	2nd	3rd	4th	5th
first	second	third	fourth	fifth

6th **sixth**	10th **tenth**	14th **fourteenth**	18th **eighteenth**
7th **seventh**	11th **eleventh**	15th **fifteenth**	19th **nineteenth**
8th **eighth**	12th **twelfth**	16th **sixteenth**	20th **twentieth**
9th **ninth**	13th **thirteenth**	17th **seventeenth**	21st **twenty-first**

8 Ask and answer.

When's your birthday?

15th September.

5

9 **Look, listen and say.** TR: A9

The kite is **mine.**

The coat is **yours.**

The ball is **his.**

The bat is **hers.**

The grapes are **ours.**

The pencils are **yours.**

The game is **theirs.**

10 **Look around your classroom.** Ask and answer.

Whose pencil is this?

It's yours.

11 Read and write.

me

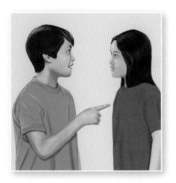

you

him

her

it

us

you

them

1. John! Jenny! I've got some lunch for ____you_____.

2. Hi, Dad. Can I help _____?

3. Thanks, Jenny. Where's your brother? I can't see _____.

4. Mum is over there. Maybe he's with _____.

5. Go and get _____. It's time to eat!

6. I love chicken sandwiches! Pass _____ that big one, please!

7. Dad, we want to play football. Would you like to come with

   _____?

8. OK, where's the ball? Oh, I can see _____!

7

Unit 1
A Helping Hand

In this unit, I will ...
• talk about caring for others.
• describe daily routines.
• talk about how often people do things.

Look and tick.

This is a baby

○ zebra.

○ lion.

○ tiger.

The woman is

○ frowning.

○ smiling.

○ crying.

Zookeeper feeds tiger cub,
Gianyar, Indonesia

We care for each other and we care for animals. We help in many different ways.

help

carry

hug

teach

hold hands

pick up

give my pet a bath

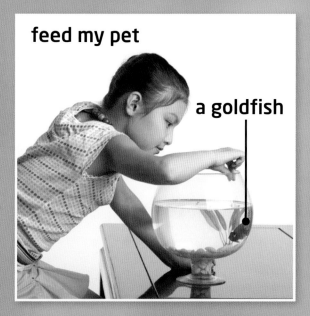

feed my pet

a goldfish

protect

take care of my pet

a hamster

3 **Work with a friend.**
Ask and answer.

What do you like doing?

I like taking care of my goldfish.

11

4 **Listen.** Read and sing. TR: A12

Taking Care

I love taking care of my pets.
I love taking care of my family.
I love taking care of them all.
I'm happy to help so many!

I love taking care of my pets.
I love picking them up and holding them, too.
But before I can play with my pets,
I've got some work to do.

I have to comb my cat, feed my dog,
protect my bird and pick up my frog.
I have to wash my goat, brush my horse
And I can't forget to give my snake a bath, of course.

CHORUS

I love taking care of my family.
I love hugging them, too.
But before I get to play with my family,
I've got some work to do.

I have to read to my sister,
take care of my brothers
and hold hands with my grandmother.
I have to teach my brothers their 1, 2, 3s
and carry my family's new baby.

I love taking care of my pets.
I love taking care of my family.
After all my work is done,
I can have some fun. With my
cat and dog, bird and frog,
goat and horse and my snake, of course!
My sisters and my brothers, my grandmother
and even my family's new baby!

5 **Sing again and hold up pictures.**

13

What does she do **before** breakfast? She gets dressed **before** breakfast.
What does he do **after** school? He feeds his bird **after** school.

6 **Work with a friend.** Look at the pictures.
Make sentences.

BEFORE SCHOOL

AFTER SCHOOL

1. _He brushes his teeth before school._

2. _____

3. _____

4. _____

5. _____

6. _____

7 **What about you?** Write about what you do before and after school.

Before school	After school

8 **Work with a friend.** Ask and answer.

What do you do after breakfast?

I brush my teeth.

9 Listen and say. Tick **T** for *True* or **F** for *False*. TR: A14

have a shower

make my bed

come home

have a snack

do my homework

1. She has a shower at six thirty. (T) (✓F)

2. She makes her bed at eight fifteen. (T) (F)

3. She comes home at three twenty-five. (T) (F)

4. She has a snack at four forty-five. (T) (F)

5. She does her homework at five o'clock. (T) (F)

10 Stick and write times.
Work with a friend.

What time do you have a shower?

I have a shower at 7.45.

I **never** have lunch at 12.30.   I **sometimes** have lunch at 12.30.
I **usually** have lunch at 12.30.   I **always** have lunch at 12.30.

11 **Read and write.**

never ○○○   sometimes ●○○
usually ●●○   always ●●●

	🚿 8.15	⚽ 6.30	🧹 6.30	🧺 8.45
Meena	●○○	○○○	●●○	●●●
Tom	●●●	●○○	○○○	●●○

1. **Meena**   I _____never_____ play football at 6.30.

2. **Tom**   I _____ have a shower at 8.15.

3. **Meena**   I _____ help at home at 6.30.

4. **Tom**   I _____ go to bed at 8.45.

5. **Meena**   I _____ have a shower at 8.15.

12 **Play a game.** Cut out the game board and cards on page 159.
Play with a friend.

I usually make my bed in the morning.

I always make my bed in the morning.

So we're different.

My Mum, the Aeroplane

There are not many whooping cranes in the world. People have to protect these birds and help them to live safely. There are some special places in North America where people protect the whooping crane's eggs. They then take care of the baby cranes.

These cranes do not have mothers to follow, so they follow a scientist who wears a crane suit and they walk with a small aeroplane. They listen to the aeroplane, too. Soon they are happy to fly with the aeroplanes–they think the aeroplane is their mother!

Before the weather gets cold, cranes have to fly to warm places. They do not have a mother to teach them where to go, so they follow an aeroplane. Some journeys last more than 70 days!

And in the spring, when the weather is warm again, they fly back on their own. These birds can then teach a new generation of young cranes where to go next year.

All birds come from dinosaurs!

Wingspans

244 cm. (8 ft.)

46 cm. (1.5 ft.)

parrot

whooping crane

14 **Read.** Underline the incorrect word and write the correct one.

1. People protect the whooping crane's eggs

   in some special places in <u>South</u> America. _____North_____

2. The cranes follow the aeroplane to cold places. _____

3. Some of their journeys last more than 70 weeks. _____

4. In the summer, the cranes fly back on their own. _____

5. The wingspan of a whooping crane is six feet. _____

15 **Read.** Number the sentences in order.

[ ] The cranes fly with aeroplanes to warm places.

[1] People protect the crane's eggs.

[ ] The cranes walk with aeroplanes.

[ ] The cranes fly back on their own.

[ ] Baby cranes come out of the eggs.

16 **Work with a friend.**
Talk about the reading.

There are not many whooping cranes in the world.

The cranes follow aeroplanes to warm places.

19

17 **Read.** Read the email. Naomi uses *before, after* and *first* to show the order that her father does things. Underline these words.

« » ⊞ 📶

Dear Carlos,

My dad's job is really cool. He is a zookeeper! He takes care of the elephants. He gets up at 6.30. After breakfast he always goes to see the elephants. They are called Archie and Tina. He usually gives the elephants a bath first! He uses a lot of water. After that he feeds them. They eat lots of potatoes and carrots. Before lunch he cleans the elephant barn. Sometimes, in the afternoon, he walks with the elephants and helps them to exercise.

He loves his new job. I would like to visit him at the zoo!

Naomi

18 **Write.** Think about someone who takes care of animals or people. Write about his or her day.

19 **Work in groups of three.** Read your writing to your group. Listen. Take turns. Complete the table.

Name	Who?	What do they do?

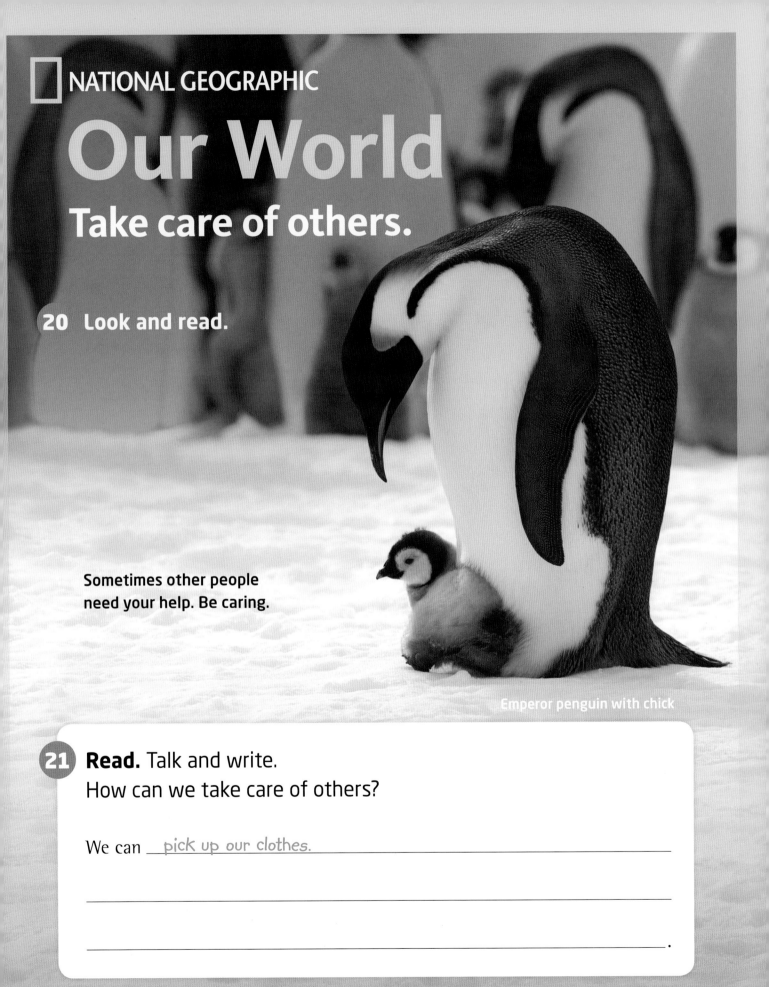

NATIONAL GEOGRAPHIC

Our World

Take care of others.

20 Look and read.

Sometimes other people need your help. Be caring.

Emperor penguin with chick

21 **Read.** Talk and write.
How can we take care of others?

We can ___pick up our clothes._____

_____

_____.

22 **Make a collage.** Show ways people care.

Cut out a big circle.

Collect and draw pictures that show caring.

Glue the pictures to cover the circle.

Tell the class about your collage.

They care for their families!

My Caring Collage

Now I can ...

- ◯ talk about caring for others.

- ◯ describe daily routines.

- ◯ talk about how many times people do things.

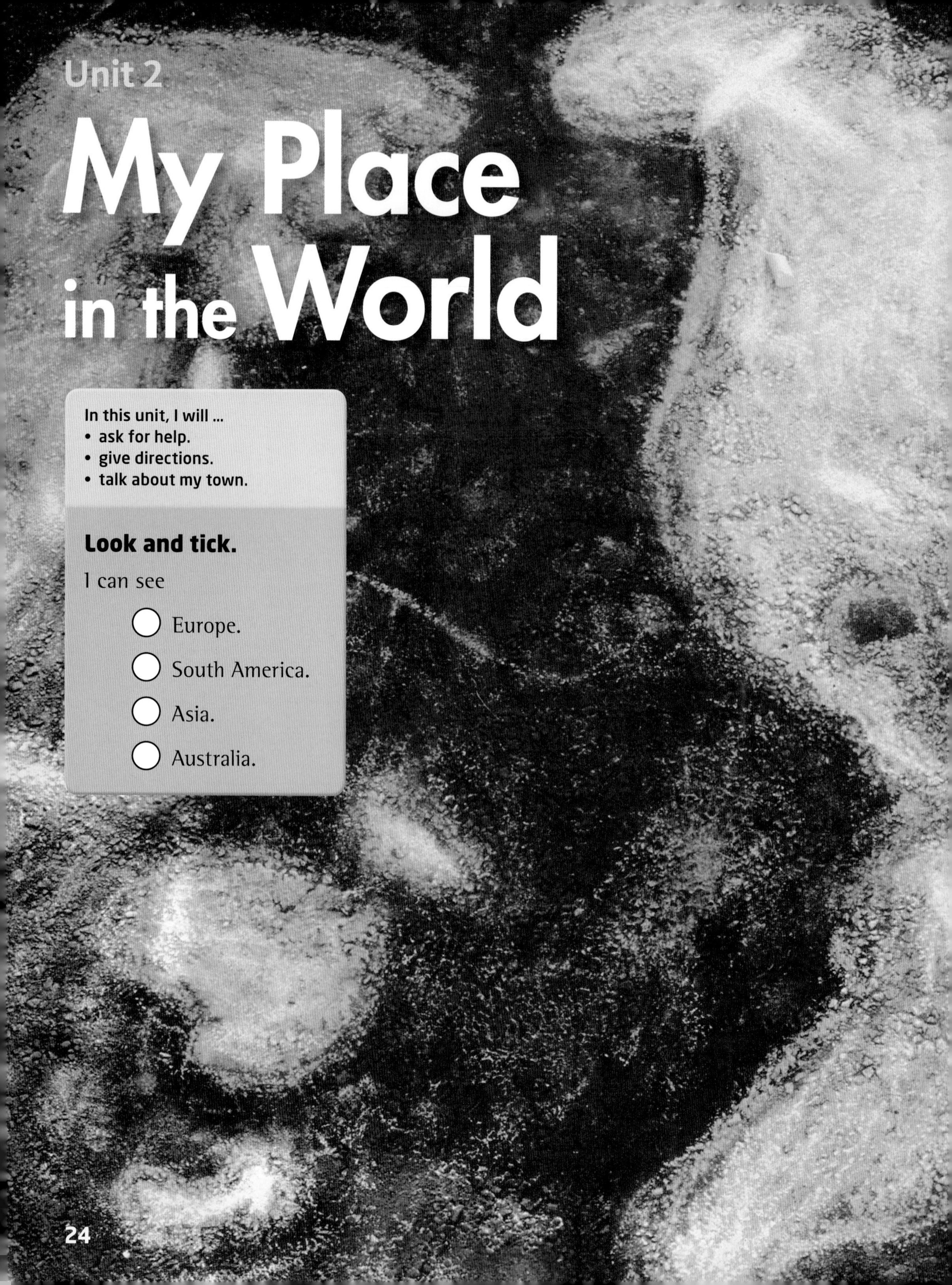

My Place in the World

In this unit, I will …
• ask for help.
• give directions.
• talk about my town.

Look and tick.

1 can see

○ Europe.

○ South America.

○ Asia.

○ Australia.

2 **Listen and say.** TR: A18

Some people live in big towns. Other people live in small villages. In both, there are interesting places to go. Look at all the places in this town!

a hospital

a post office

a bakery

a museum

a restaurant

a park

a supermarket

a chemist's

a train station

a cinema

a toy shop

a police station

3 **Work with a friend.** Describe and guess. Use these words.

a doctor	a swing	food	films
paintings	bread	a police officer	

You can get medicine here.

It's a chemist's!

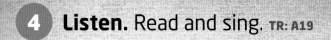

A Great New Town

Can I help you? You look lost.
Can I help you find your way?
Can I help you? You look lost.
Can I help you today?

I'm new in town. I think I'm lost.
Can you help me find my way?
I'm new in town.
Can you help me with my busy day?

Where are the post office, the toy shop,
the supermarket and the park?
Where's the bakery?
Where's the library?
Where are the zoo, the school and the
swimming pool?

CHORUS

I can help you. You're not lost.
I can help you find your way.
I can help you. You're not lost.
I can help you today.

Here's the post office.
Here's the toy shop, the supermarket
and the park.
Here's the bakery, the library, the zoo,
the school, the swimming pool
and the cinema, too!

I can help you. You're not lost.
I can help you today.
I can help you find your way, and you'll be OK
in your great new town today!

Thank you for helping me to find my way.
Thank you for helping me with my busy day
in my great new town today!
In my great new town today!

5 **Sing again and hold up pictures.**

Can you **help** me, please?   Of course. How **can I help**?

6 **Read.** Look at the map. Match the sentences.

1. Can you help me, please?
2. Where's the park?
3. Where's the toy shop?
4. Where's the museum?
5. Where's the cinema?

a. It's on the corner of Main Street. It's next to the bakery.
b. It's opposite the supermarket.
c. It's behind the hospital.
d. Yes, of course. How can I help?
e. It's between the hospital and the supermarket.

7 **Write more questions about the town.** Work with a friend. Ask and answer.

8 **What about you?** Think about where *you* live. Work with a friend. Ask and answer.

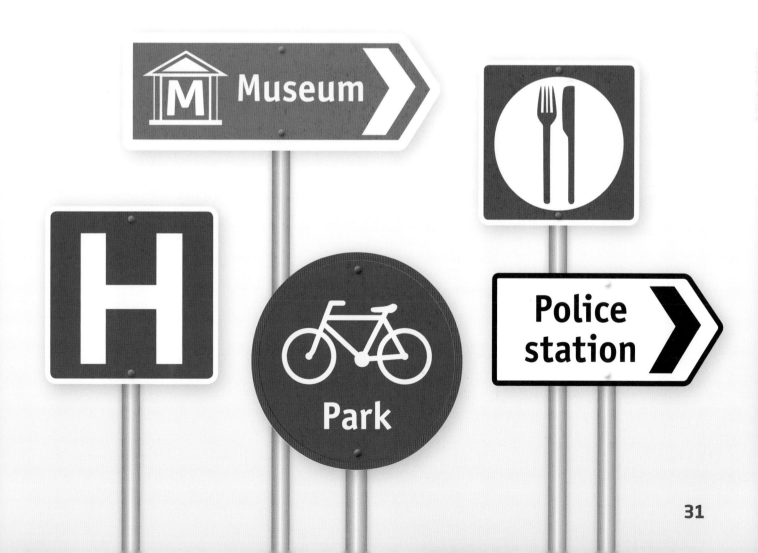

9 Listen and say.
Read and write. TR: A21

a library

a swimming pool

a zoo

a shopping centre

a stadium

1. Min wants to go to the _zoo_____.
   She loves the crocodiles and the monkeys.

2. Aziz wants to go to the _____.
   He likes seeing his favourite football team.

3. Janica wants to go to the _____.
   She likes swimming.

4. Mounira wants to go to the _____.
   She wants to buy some new clothes.

5. Leo wants to go the _____.
   He wants to read some books.

10 Listen and stick. TR: A22

Monday	Tuesday	Wednesday	Thursday	Friday

32

How **do** I **get** to the chemist's?

Go straight on ↑.
Turn left ← at Third Avenue.
Turn right → at the supermarket.

11 **Look at the map below.** Follow and write.

1. How do I get to the _____? Turn left at Summer Street. Go straight on. Turn right at Spring Street. It's next to the shopping centre.

2. How _____? Go straight on along Green Street. Turn left at Middle Street. It's on the corner of Second Avenue.

3. How _____? Go straight on along Green Street. Turn right at Middle Street. Turn left at Black Street. It's next to the swimming pool.

4. How _____? Turn left at Summer Street. Turn right at Second Avenue. Go straight on to Sunny Street. It's next to the bookshop.

12 **Play a game.** Cut out the cards on page 161. Play with a friend. Ask for directions. Take turns.

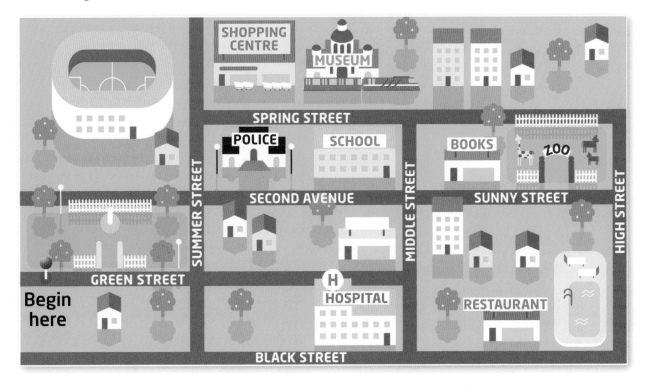

Eye in the Sky

681 km.
(423 mi.)

Satellites are machines in space that circle the Earth. They help us to talk to people on the other side of the planet. They can also study the planet's weather. This satellite is called GeoEye 1. It is the same size as a big car. It takes photos of our planet. These pictures can show our continents and oceans. They can show our streets and houses, too!

On the Internet there are many photos and maps of the Earth. We can use these images to help us to explore our world.

This is a photo of the world. You can see the seven continents. Do you know their names?

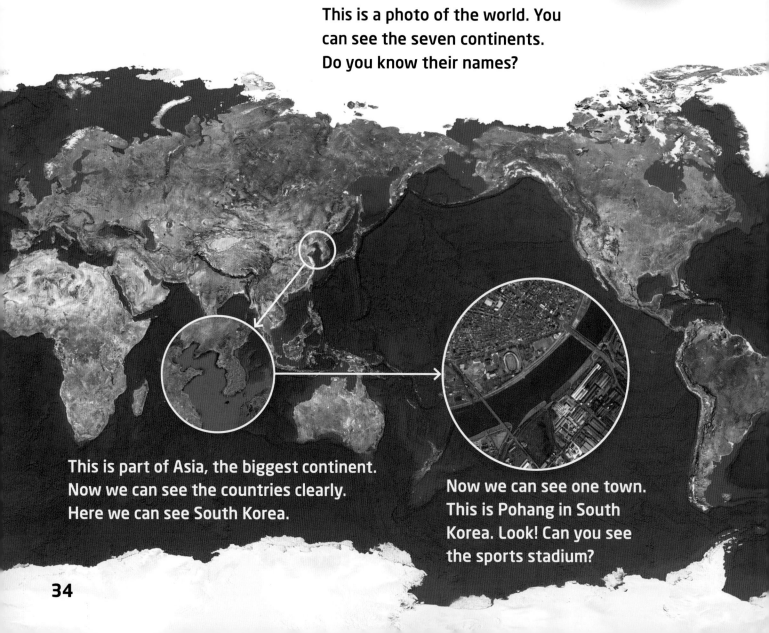

This is part of Asia, the biggest continent. Now we can see the countries clearly. Here we can see South Korea.

Now we can see one town. This is Pohang in South Korea. Look! Can you see the sports stadium?

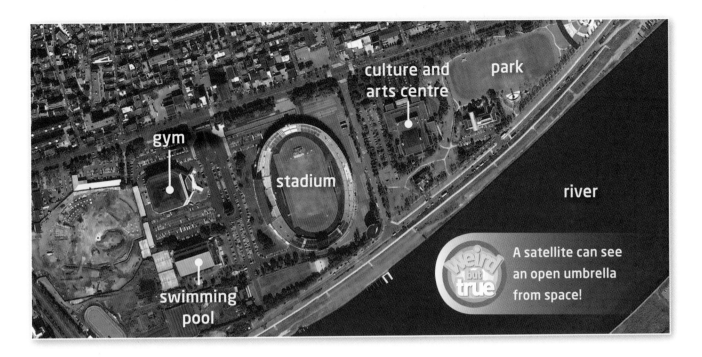

culture and arts centre
park
gym
stadium
river
swimming pool

A satellite can see an open umbrella from space!

Weird but true

---

14 **Look at the satellite map.** Tick **T** for *True* or **F** for *False*.

1. The gym is next to the river. Ⓣ Ⓕ

2. The stadium is between the gym and the culture and arts centre. Ⓣ Ⓕ

3. The park is next to the gym. Ⓣ Ⓕ

4. The gym is near the swimming pool. Ⓣ Ⓕ

---

15 **Read and write.** Write the words in order from small to big.

continent   country   house   planet   street   town

small _____ _____ _____

_____ _____ _____ big

---

16 **Work with a friend.** Talk about your town. You can use a photo or map.

Look! There's the shopping centre.

Yes, it's next to the park.

17 Read. We can use the word *and* to connect two ideas. Underline the sentences with *and* as you read.

My special place in the world

My name is Jan and I live in a town in Poland called Kazimierz Dolny. It's a lovely town.

There is a hill by the town. You can walk up the hill and you can see the whole town. I think it's beautiful, and it's very quiet. It's my favourite place.

My second favourite place is the bakery! My town is famous for its special bread. The bakery makes bread in the shape of a chicken. It's delicious!

18 Write. Write about your special place in the world.

_____

_____

_____

_____

19 Work in groups of three. Read your writing to your group. Listen. Take turns. Complete the table.

Name	Favourite place

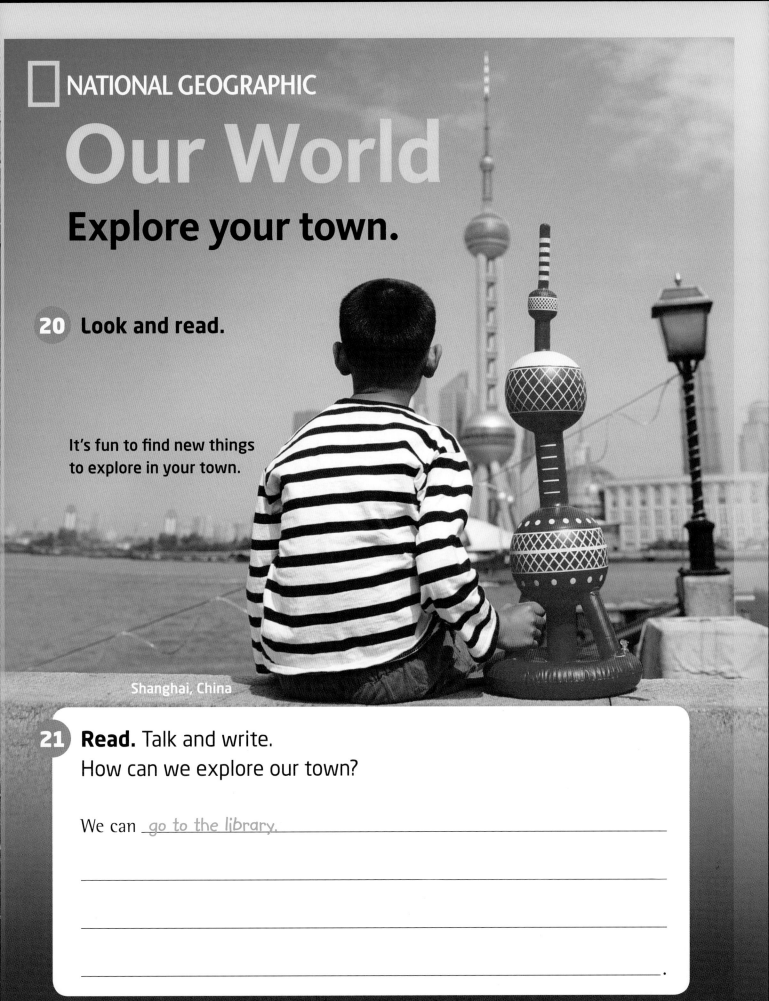

Our World

Explore your town.

20 **Look and read.**

It's fun to find new things to explore in your town.

Shanghai, China

21 **Read.** Talk and write.
How can we explore our town?

We can _go to the library._

22 **Make *My World* circles.**

Cut out six circles of different sizes.

On the other circles, do the same for *My Neighbourhood, My Town, My Country, My Continent* and *My World.*

On the smallest circle, draw a picture of your house and write *My House.*

Taking care, join the circles together with a split pin.

Now I can ...

○ ask for help.

○ give directions.

○ talk about my town.

Unit 3
On the Move!

In this unit, I will ...
- identify different kinds of transport.
- describe ways of travelling.
- compare and contrast.

Tick T for *True* or F for *False*.

The city

1. is very quiet.   T F

2. has a lot of cars.   T F

3. is very busy.   T F

Taksim Square, Istanbul

Different kinds of transport help us move around. We can travel in the sky, on water or on land. Which is your favourite?

a sailing boat

an aeroplane

a helicopter

a ferry

a bus

an underground train

a hot-air balloon

a ship

a scooter

a scooter

a taxi

a motorbike

3 **Work with a friend.** Describe and guess.

It's in the sky.

Is it an aeroplane?

43

4 **Listen.** Read and sing. TR: A27

How Do You Get to School?

How do you get to school?
How do you get to school?
How do you get to school?
How do you get to school?

I get the bus to school.
I do, too.
I ride my bike to school.
I do, too.

CHORUS

My mum drives me to school.
My mum does, too.
I walk to school.
I do, too.

CHORUS

Listen and I'll tell you
Listen and I'll tell you
Listen and I'll tell you
how I get to School.

I get a ferry to school. Yes, I do.
I get a ferry to school. Do you get one, too?

I get the train to school. Yes, I do.
I get the train to school. Do you get it, too?

CHORUS

5 **Work in a group.** Act out how you get to school. Your group guesses.

I ride my scooter to school.	**I do, too.**
I get the bus to school.	**I don't.** I walk.
My brother rides his bike to school.	**My brother does, too.**
My sister rides her skateboard to school.	**My sister doesn't.** She walks.

6 **Read.** Write a sentence with *do, don't, does* or *doesn't.*

1. I get the bus to school.

_____

2. My sister rides her bike every day.

_____

3. I ride my scooter after school.

_____

4. My cousins go on holiday by aeroplane every summer.

_____

5. I take my dog to the park every day.

_____

7 **Marco is doing a survey.** Listen and tick. TR: A29

Name	Scooter	Bus	Walk	Bicycle
Miguel				
Ken				
Fernanda				
Rosie				
Thomas				
Eman				

8 **Look.** Write sentences about Marco's survey.

Thomas walks to school.
Fernanda doesn't. She gets the bus.

How do you get to school?

I ride my bike.

9 **Work with a friend.** How do you get to school? Talk about you and your friends.

47

10 Listen and say. Read and write. TR: A30

get on

pedal uphill

coast downhill

get off

park

1. After school, I _____ my bike and I ride home. I can ride home in 15 minutes.

2. I sometimes _____. I get tired, but at the top of the hill you can see the whole town!

3. I _____, too. It can be very fast. You have to be careful.

4. When I get home, I _____ my bike and _____ it. I'm usually hungry, so I have a snack.

11 Listen and stick. TR: A31

1	2	3	4	5

My mother gets the bus to work, **but** my father rides his bicycle.

12 Look at the pictures and complete.

1. The boy rides his scooter to school,

   but the girl rides her bike to school.

2. The girl has breakfast at eight o'clock,

   _____

3. The boy has got a pet rabbit,

   _____

4. He wants to be a singer,

   _____

5. The girl likes spaghetti for lunch,

   _____

13 Play a game. Cut out the cards on page 163. Play with a friend. Make sentences about the cards. Find and keep pairs.

Jenny wants to fly in a hot air balloon. Jenny likes cereal for breakfast. No pair. Your turn!

Pair! Jenny likes playing tennis on Saturdays, but Sam likes playing football on Saturdays.

Hot-Air Balloons

It's always exciting to see a colourful hot-air balloon in the sky—but here there are hundreds! In October every year, there is an International Balloon Fiesta in Albuquerque, USA. About 600 balloons are up in the sky at the same time. And many of these are shaped like animals, fish and even spaceships!

How do hot-air balloons fly? When the balloon is on the ground, people light gas to make a small fire. This heats the air in the balloon. Hot air always goes up. So the balloon goes up slowly into the air. The pilot stands in the basket and lights the gas to go higher. The wind blows the balloon along.

Usually there is a group of people on the ground called the 'chase team'. They are in a van, and they follow the balloon. They use a radio to talk to the pilot. The pilot looks for a safe place to land the balloon and tells the chase team where to go. Then the chase team takes the balloon and the pilot back home!

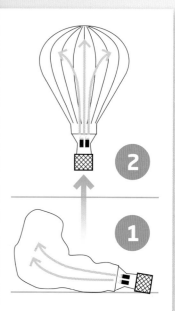

15 **Read.** Tick **T** for *True* or **F** for *False*.

1. There is an International Balloon Fiesta every year. (T)✓ (F)

2. Hot air never goes up. (T) (F)

3. Balloons are always round. (T) (F)

4. The basket is where the pilot stands. (T) (F)

5. The chase team talks to the pilot with a radio. (T) (F)

16 **Read.** Write the sentences in order.

The wind blows the balloon along.

↓

People light a fire to heat the air in the balloon.

↓

The pilot lands the balloon safely.

↓

The balloon goes up into the air.

↓

The pilot talks to the chase team.

17 **Work with a friend.** Look at the photographs from the balloon festival. Describe your favourite balloon.

Which balloon do you like?

I like the red balloon!

The first passengers in a hot-air balloon were a chicken, a duck and a sheep!

51

18 **Read.** We can use the word *but* to show that two connected ideas are different. Underline the sentences with the word *but* as you read.

Catch the bus in Curitiba!

My city of Curitiba, Brazil, is famous for its bus system. It is called the BRT. There are more than a thousand buses in our city. There are lots of cars and lorries on the roads, but the buses use a special lane. They can move quickly. In some parts of the city, you can catch a bus every 90 seconds. Many buses are a normal size, but some of the buses are very long. They carry a lot of people. The buses are modern and some of the bus stops are, too. At these stops, people can get on and off the bus in 15 seconds.

19 **Write.** Write about your favourite kind of transport where you live.

20 **Work in groups of three.** Read your writing to your group. Listen. Take turns. Complete the table.

Name	Transport

NATIONAL GEOGRAPHIC
Our World

Be safe on the street.

21 Look and read.

Stop.
Look both ways.
Listen.

Busy intersection, Hanoi, Vietnam

22 Read. Talk and write.
How can we be safe on the street?

We can _look both ways before we cross the road._

_____

_____

_____ .

Make a class bar chart about favourite kinds of transport.

Cut out a 10 cm. (4 inch) square piece of paper.

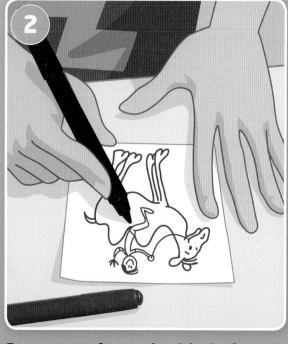

Draw your favourite kind of transport.

With your class, make a bar chart for your pictures.

Glue your pictures in place.

Our class really likes bikes. It's our favourite kind of transport.

Now I can ...

- ○ identify different kinds of transport.
- ○ describe ways of travelling.
- ○ compare and contrast.

OUR FAVOURITE TRANSPORT

aeroplane walking bicycle helicopter sailing boat camel train motorbike

Review

5.00 p.m.

BAKERY MUSEUM TOY SHOP

6.45 a.m.

Finish

ZOO

8.15 p.m.

7.20 a.m.

There isn't any wind! Go back two spaces!

There's a lot of wind! Go forward two spaces!

8.15 a.m.

LIBRARY

ZOO CINEMA CINEMA

7.30 a.m.

Work with a friend. Use a coin.
Heads = 2 spaces, Tails = 1 space.
Look. Ask and answer.

Heads! One, two.
Where's the museum?

Our Senses

In this unit, I will …
• talk about the senses.
• talk about how things look, feel, taste, sound and smell.
• talk about the past.

Look and tick.

This person is

○ touching the jellyfish.

○ looking at the jellyfish.

○ smelling the jellyfish.

Diver with jellyfish

2 **Listen and say.** TR: A35

We use our eyes, ears, nose, tongue and skin to learn about the world around us.

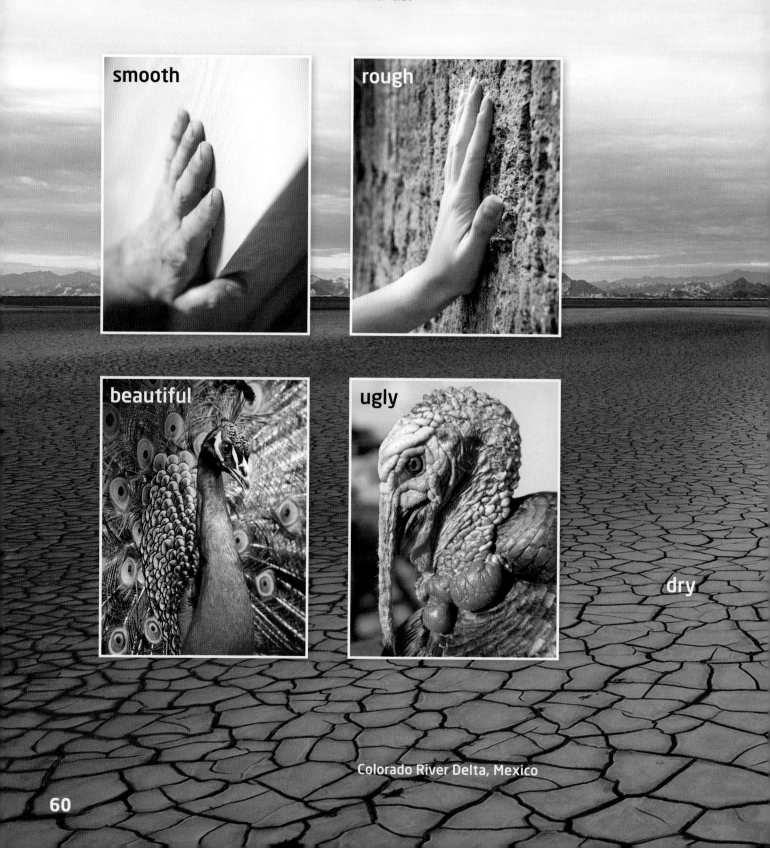

smooth

rough

beautiful

ugly

dry

Colorado River Delta, Mexico

sticky

hard

soft

terrible

delicious

quiet

loud

3 **Work with a friend.** Describe. Listen and guess.

a cake	an elephant	a flower
a leaf	a rabbit	a rock	a tomato

It's small. It's soft. I think it's beautiful. What is it?

A rabbit!

61

Our Senses

How does the cake taste?
It tastes sweet.
How does a kitten feel?
It feels soft.

Let's count our senses, 1, 2, 3, 4, 5!
Listen.
Look.
Feel.
Taste.
Smell.
It's great to be alive!

Polar bear mum hugs her cubs,
Manitoba, Canada

How does a drum sound?
It sounds loud.
How does a flower smell?
It smells nice.

CHORUS

How does a garden look?
It looks beautiful.
How does a hug feel?
It feels great!

CHORUS

5 **Work in a small group.** Name an object.
Take turns. Say how it is.

The soup **smells** great.   The music **sounds** terrible.
The flowers **look** beautiful.   The baby rabbit **feels** soft.
How **does** the chicken **taste**?   It **tastes** delicious.

6 **Write sentences.** Use these words.

sticky	nice	old	rough	smooth	terrible

1. The cake _____tastes nice_____.

2. The dog _____.

3. The house _____.

4. The glue _____.

5. The rock _____.

6. The phone _____.

7 **What about you?** Look around you. Write true sentences.

1. _My desk feels smooth._

2. _____

3. _____

4. _____

Now imagine you are outside. Write more sentences.

1. _The mountains look beautiful._

2. _____

3. _____

4. _____

8 **Listen and say.** Read and write. TR: A38

salty

bitter

sweet

sour

spicy

1. This lemon isn't sweet. It's ___sour_____.

2. I don't like honey. I don't like _____ things.

3. These crisps make me thirsty. They're very _____.

4. I like chilli peppers. They're _____.

5. I don't like the taste of coffee. It's very _____.

9 **Listen and stick.** Work with a friend. Check your answers. TR: A39

> Number 1 is spicy.

> Yes. It's a chilli pepper.

1   2   3   4   5

How**'s** the ice cream? | It's delicious!
How **was** the ice cream? | It **was** delicious. More, please!
How **were** the biscuits? | They **were** great. Can I have one more, please?

10 **Read and write.**

1. That ice cream ___was___ delicious. I would like some more!

2. The music _____ loud, but now it's quiet.

3. The flowers _____ beautiful before. They are ugly now.

4. Well done! That song _____ beautiful.

5. The glue _____ sticky, but now it is dry.

11 **Play a game.** Make the wheels on page 165.
Spin and make sentences. Play with a friend.

Flowers, were. The flowers were beautiful, but now they aren't.

Well done. My turn. *Music, are.* No match!

Amazing Animal Senses

Many animals can see, hear, smell, taste and touch – but they do it in a different way from humans.

Imagine you have to walk on your dinner to taste it! Well, a butterfly does – it tastes with its feet!

People use the ends of their fingers to touch. Seals use their whiskers. Their sense of touch is amazing. They can feel fish through the water 180 metres (590 feet) away.

whisker

Spiders do not have ears. They hear using hundreds of small hairs on their legs.

We can smell delicious food in front of a restaurant. But we can't smell food that is in a different town! Bears have a fantastic sense of smell. They can smell things that are 32 kilometres (20 miles) away.

Chameleons can see very well – look at their eyes! One eye looks up, and the other eye looks down. They can see all around them.

13 **Read.** Tick **T** for *True* or **F** for *False*.

1. Spiders use ears to hear.   (T) (F✓)

2. Bears can't smell very well.   (T) (F)

3. Butterflies taste with their feet.   (T) (F)

4. Seals use their whiskers to feel fish in the water.   (T) (F)

5. Chameleons can look up and down at the same time.   (T) (F)

14 **Read the text again.** Write.

Animal	Sense	Why is it unusual?
butterfly	taste	It uses its feet.

15 **Work with a friend.** Talk about other animals you know.

A worm can taste
with its whole body.

I think dogs can
hear very well.

Bats can't see
very well.

16 **Read.** We can use *and* to show that two connected ideas are similar. We can use *but* to show that two connected ideas are different. When we can choose between two connected ideas, we use *or.* Underline the sentences with *or.*

Summer is my favourite season. The weather is hot and we do lots of activities outside. At the weekend we visit our grandparents, or sometimes we go to the river with my cousin.

At my grandparents' house we sit outside and play cards, or we play with their pet dog, Charlie. My grandma loves flowers. They look beautiful and they smell great, too.

There is a river near my cousins' house and we swim there sometimes. The water's cold, but I love it! We eat fruit, or sometimes we eat ice cream. My brother likes chocolate ice cream, but strawberry is my favourite!

17 **Write.** Write about your summer. Use *or* to show choices.

18 **Work in groups of three.** Read your writing to your group. Listen. Take turns. Complete the table.

Name	Choice 1		Choice 2
		or	

Our World

Enjoy the world through your senses.

19 **Look and read.**

Take time to enjoy
the world around you.
Use all your senses.

Iguazu Falls, Argentina and Brazil

20 **Read.** Talk and write. How do you use your senses
in the winter, spring, summer and autumn?

Winter _My hands feel the cold snow._

Spring

Summer

Autumn

21 **Make a class book of Five Senses poems.** Think of an experience when you used your five senses. Write about it.

Use paper to plan your work for each of the senses.

Write sentences.

Draw pictures.

Write your name.

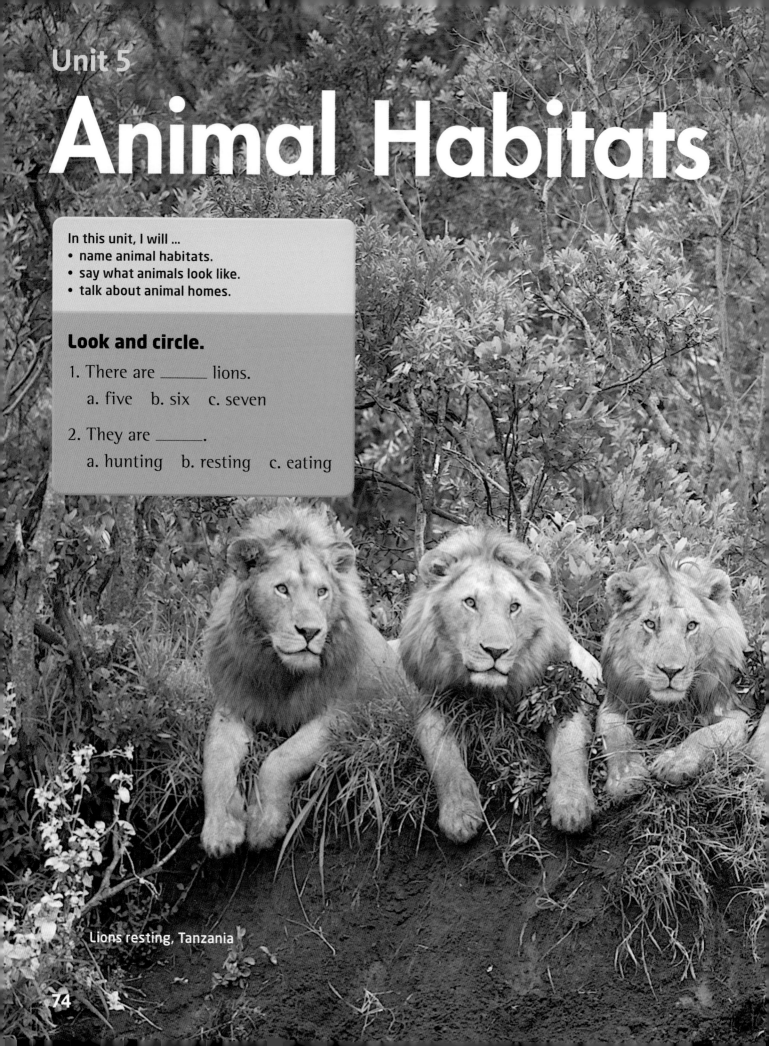

Animal Habitats

In this unit, I will …
- name animal habitats.
- say what animals look like.
- talk about animal homes.

Look and circle.

1. There are _____ lions.
   a. five   b. six   c. seven

2. They are _____.
   a. hunting   b. resting   c. eating

Lions resting, Tanzania

1 **Listen and read.** TR: B2

2 **Listen and say.** TR: B3

We all need a place to live. We live in houses or flats in our neighbourhood. Animals and plants have a place to live, too. This place is called their habitat.

a forest

ice

a web

grasslands

a desert

Ténéré Desert, Niger

wetlands

a hive

a cave

underground

mud

a rainforest

an island

a nest

snow

3 **Work with a friend.** Ask and answer.

Where do camels live?

They live in the desert.

Why? Because

Why has a giraffe got a long, long neck?
Why?
Why?
Because it eats leaves at the tops of the trees.

I want to know why.
I want to know why.
Why?
Because I want to know why!

Why has a frog got strong legs?
Why?
Why?
Because it hops, swims and jumps.

CHORUS

78

Animals are amazing.
They can do so many things.
And I've got just one thing to say.
Why?

Why has a polar bear got white fur?
Why?
Why?
Because it lives in ice and snow.

CHORUS

5 **Work in a group.** Act out and describe an animal. Your group guesses the animal. Take turns.

GRAMMAR TR: B5

Why does a giraffe eat leaves
at the tops of trees?   **Because** it's got a long neck.
Why are kangaroos so great?   **Because** they can jump so far!
Why don't you like penguins?   **Because** they look silly and they can't fly!

6 **Match.**

1. Why have leopards got spots?

a. Because they eat meat.

2. Why does a polar bear cover its black nose?

b. Because they need to hide in the trees.

3. Why have crocodiles got sharp teeth?

c. Because they can't fly and they need to run fast.

4. Why have owls got big eyes?

d. Because it wants to hide in the snow.

5. Why have ostriches got long legs?

e. Because they need to see at night.

7 **Ask and answer.** Work with a friend.
Talk about these animals.

monkey   penguin   rabbit   tiger   panda

elephant   parrot   octopus   spider

I don't like spiders.

Why don't you like spiders?

Because they are ugly and scary!

8 **Work in groups of three.** Talk about your friend.

She doesn't like spiders because she thinks they are ugly and scary.

9 Listen and say. Write the animals in the correct groups. TR: B6

a tongue

fur

horns

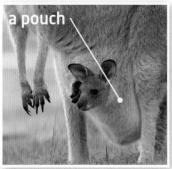
a pouch

wings

| cat | ~~parrot~~ | polar bear | penguin | monkey |
| duck | rabbit | kangaroo | butterfly | goat |

pouch	fur	wings	horns
		parrot	

10 Work with a friend. Guess and stick.

This animal is big and white. It lives in the snow. It's got sharp claws.

It's a polar bear!

1   2   3   4   5

Giraffes use their long tongues **to clean** their ears.
Goats use their horns **to fight**.

11 Read and match.

1. Zebras use their black and white fur   a. to carry their babies.

2. Cats use their tongues   b. to eat meat.

3. Kangaroos use their pouches   c. to clean their fur.

4. Elephants use their long trunks   d. to swim in the sea.

5. Tigers use their sharp teeth   e. to shower.

6. Penguins use their wings   f. to hide in the grasslands.

12 Play a game. Cut out the cubes on page 167. Work with a friend. Make sentences.

Dogs use their trunks to drink water.

That's not true! Elephants use their trunks to drink water! Dogs haven't got trunks!

83

Amazing Rainforests

Rainforests are warm, wet forests. They are in countries near the Equator – in Central America, South America, Africa, Southeast Asia and Australia. Rainforests are important. They are homes for millions of animals and plants. The plants here make a lot of the oxygen that people in the world need to live.

A RAINFOREST HAS FOUR PARTS:

Emergent
In this part, you can see the tops of very tall trees. They are sometimes 60 metres (200 feet) tall! Many different birds, butterflies and other insects live here.

Canopy
In this part of the forest, the trees have many leaves. Birds, spiders, tree frogs, monkeys and snakes live here.

Understorey
In this part of the forest, it is dark, wet and cool. There aren't many plants. Why? Because plants need light to live. Snakes and lizards live here. Jaguars like to live in this part, too!

Forest floor
In this part, there are many insects and spiders – some spiders are as big as plates! There are many large animals. And people live here, too!

Howler monkeys are very, very loud. You can hear them from 5 kilometres (3 miles) away.

14 **Read.** Circle the correct words.

1. Rainforests are in countries (near) / **far from** the Equator.

2. Plants make a lot of **oxygen** / **water.**

3. Plants need **light** / **oxygen** to live.

4. Many **birds** / **leopards** live in the top part of the rainforest.

5. Many large animals live on the **forest floor** / **tops of trees.**

15 **Read.** Complete the table. Use these words. Use some words more than once.

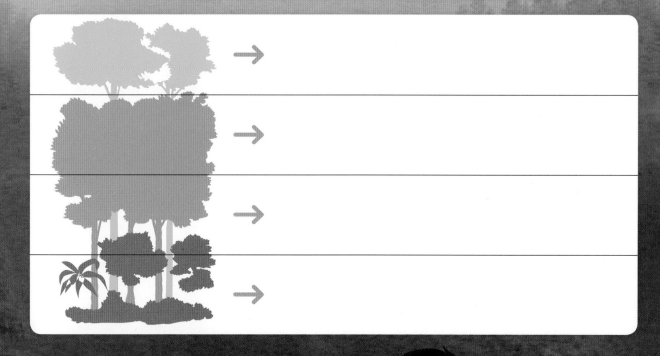

dark   sunny   monkeys   snakes   birds   spiders   large animals

16 **Work with a friend.** Talk about the different parts of the rainforest.

There are gorillas in this part.

17 **Read.** Read about Mounira's animal. Underline words that tell you what the animal looks like. Write the name of the animal.

My name is Mounira. I live by the Nile River. This animal lives here. What is it? Can you guess?

It lives in the river. It's brown and it's got black spots on its back. It's got four short legs and a long tail. It's got big eyes on top of its head, and it uses them to see above the water. It's got a strong mouth and sharp teeth! It can walk and it can swim.

It's scary, but I like it!

Yes! It's a _____.

18 **Write.** Write about an animal you like.

19 **Work in groups of three.** Take turns to describe your animal. Listen. Complete the table.

Name	Animal	Where it lives	What it looks like

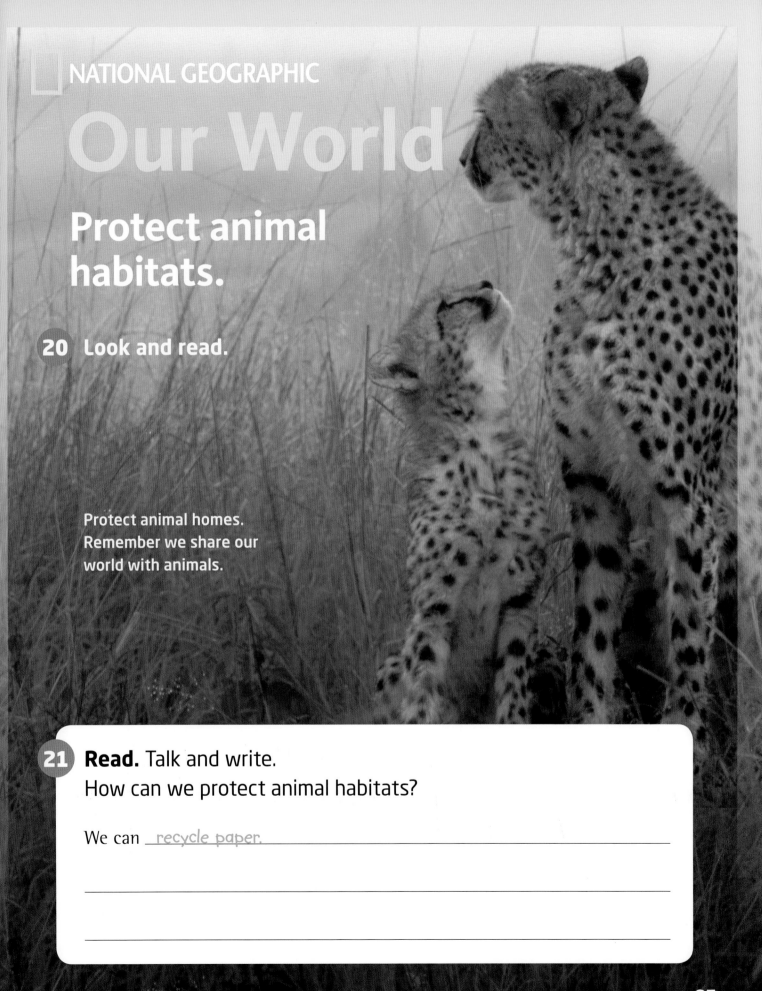

NATIONAL GEOGRAPHIC

Our World

Protect animal habitats.

20 **Look and read.**

Protect animal homes.
Remember we share our
world with animals.

21 **Read.** Talk and write.
How can we protect animal habitats?

We can _recycle paper._

22 **Make a mobile.** Choose a habitat and animals.

Choose an animal and draw it.

Research your animal's habitat. What other animals and plants live there?

Draw these animals and plants.

Hang the pictures on your mobile.

Now I can ...

- name animal habitats.
- say what animals look like.
- talk about animal homes.

What's for Dinner?

In this unit, I will …
• name foods.
• talk about quantities.
• talk about favourite meals.

Look and circle.

1. He is _____.
   a. playing   b. fishing   c. swimming

2. He is having _____ for dinner.
   a. fish   b. vegetables   c. chicken

Traditional fishing,
Mare, New Caledonia

1 **Listen and read.** TR: B9

2 **Listen and say.** TR: B10

We all love food. We can find food in shops or at the market. What's your favourite food? Let's go shopping!

a bottle of oil

a bag of rice

a loaf of bread

a jar of olives

a box of cereal

a bowl of sugar

a bunch of bananas

a glass of juice

a can of fizzy drink

a piece of cake

3 **Work with a friend.** Say what you can see. Add on to the sentence each time. Take turns.

At the market, I can see a jar of olives.

At the market, I can see a jar of olives and a loaf of bread.

Let's Go Shopping!

Let's go shopping! Let's go shopping!
Let's go shopping today.
Let's go shopping to buy some food,
then go home to put it away.

A jar of jam is no fun,
if there isn't any bread to spread it on.
A bowl of rice is very nice,
but it tastes better with some spice!

CHORUS

Let's buy some pasta at the shop,
and some sauce to put on top.
Let's buy a cake. Cake's a treat!
I like cake because it's sweet.

A bowl of pasta, a jar of spice,
a glass of juice and a cake are nice!
Let's go now. Let's buy some food.
Let's go shopping, just me and you!

CHORUS

5 **Work with a friend.**
Sing. Find and point.

Are there **any** oranges?	Yes, there are **some** in the fruit bowl.
Are there **any** bananas?	No, there aren't **any**.
Is there **any** milk?	Yes, there's **some** in the fridge.
Is there **any** bread?	No, there isn't **any**.

6 **Read.** Look and write answers.

1. Are there any tomatoes? _Yes, there are some on the table._

2. Is there any rice? _____

3. Are there any olives? _____

4. Are there any grapes? _____

5. Is there any sugar? _____

6. Is there any oil? _____

7 **Work with a friend.** Look at the food in the fridge. Ask and answer.

Is there any yoghurt?

No, there isn't any.

8 **Listen and say.** Read and write. TR: B13

money

put away

a price

compare

buy

1. Which drink is better for you? Let's _____ them.

   a. buy   b. compare   c. eat

2. Can you help me _____ the food in the fridge, please?

   a. compare   b. put away   c. buy

3. The _____ of that loaf of bread is 90 pence.

   a. price   b. money   c. smell

4. Let's _____ some milk. We haven't got any.

   a. compare   b. put away   c. buy

9 **Listen and stick.** Work with a friend. TR: B14

1   2   3   4   5

Are there any biscuits?	Yes, there are **a few**.
Is there any orange juice?	Yes, there is **a little**.

10 **Read and write.**

1. Is there any ice cream? Yes, there _____.

2. Are there any chilli peppers? Yes, there _____.

3. Is there any rice? Yes, there _____.

4. Are there any potatoes? Yes, there _____.

11 **Play a game.** Cut out the board game and the cards on page 169. Put the cards on the board. Play with a friend.

B2. Is there any sugar?

No, there isn't any sugar. A1. Are there any eggs?

Yes, there are a few. Here you are.

99

What I Eat

We all eat different things. A photographer, Peter Menzel, travels to many different countries to see what people eat. These are some of his photos. They show what each person eats in one day.

Bruce works on a beach in Australia. He's a lifeguard. He eats a bowl of cereal with a banana for breakfast, and he drinks a bottle of orange juice. He has a sandwich for lunch and meat and vegetables for dinner.

Cao is 16. She's an acrobat and works in the circus. She lives in China. She has yoghurt and fruit for breakfast. For lunch she has a bowl of rice with meat, eggs and onions. She doesn't have dinner because she performs in a show every evening.

Akbar is a bread baker. He lives in a city in Iran. He has eggs, salad and some tea for breakfast. He doesn't stop working for lunch. He has some snacks – a bunch of grapes, some tomatoes and some of his bread. He has a big dinner at home. He eats meat, rice, yoghurt and some more of his bread!

lifeguard, Australia

acrobat, China

baker, Iran

13 Read. Tick **T** for *True* or **F** for *False*.

1. Peter Menzel is a lifeguard. (T) (F✓)
2. Bruce works outside. (T) (F)
3. Akbar, Bruce and Cao live in the same country. (T) (F)
4. Cao and Akbar don't have dinner. (T) (F)
5. Akbar, Bruce and Cao all eat fruit. (T) (F)

14 Read. Complete the table.

	Bruce	Cao	Akbar
Country			
Breakfast			
Lunch			
Dinner			

15 **Work with a friend.** Look at the photos. Talk about what the people eat. What do you eat?

Weird but true

Every day, half the people in the world eat rice.

Bruce has cereal for breakfast.

I do, too!

101

16 **Read.** Read this paragraph about Marcela's favourite food. In a paragraph, the first sentence is called the *topic sentence.* It gives the reader the main idea. The other sentences are called the *body* of the paragraph. They give more information about that idea.

My favourite meal

I love many kinds of food, but I have one favourite meal! First, I have chicken soup and some bread. It's delicious! I sometimes have two bowls! After that, I have fish cakes. I eat them with salad. Yum! And I have my favourite drink – apple juice. Finally, I have a piece of cake. So that's my favourite meal.

17 **Write.** Write about your favourite meal. Then check your writing. Circle *Yes* or *No.*

Does your first sentence say what the paragraph is about?   **Yes   No**

Do the other sentences give more information about it?   **Yes   No**

18 **Work in groups of three.** Read your writing to your group. Listen. Take turns. Complete the table.

Name	Favourite meal

Our World

Eat nutritious food.

19 Look and read.

Eat fresh food. Eat good food.
Read the labels on boxes and cans.

Bear fishing, Brooks Falls, Alaska

20 **Read.** Talk and write.
What can you do to make sure you eat nutritious food?

I can eat fresh vegetables.

21 **Organise a taste-test day.** Taste food. Describe each taste.

Bring in different kinds of food.

Work with a friend. Put on a blindfold and taste the food.

Use your table to interview your friend. Write down the descriptions.

When you finish, take turns!

It's soft. It tastes salty and a bit spicy.

Now I can ...

○ name foods.

○ talk about quantities.

○ talk about favourite meals.

Work with a friend. You have three minutes to answer the questions.

One to Ten!

1. Write three animals whose name begins with c.

2.
   Are there any potatoes?   Yes, there are a

   _____!

3. Write three things you buy in bottles.

4. What lives in a hive?

5.
   Are there any bananas?   No, there aren't

   _____.

6. Why has a giraffe got a long neck?

7.
   A _____ of cereal and a

   _____ of olives, please.

8. Zebras live in the _____.

9. Write three things that are sweet.

10.
   How was the ice cream?

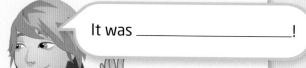

   It was _____!

Finish
Start

12 · Why ...? 1 · Why ...?
What ...?
Is ...? Is ...?
What ...? What ...?
How ...? What ...?
Is ...? Are ...?
Why ...? How ...?

Tails. Why has a camel got a hump?

Work with a friend. Use a coin.
Heads = 2 spaces, Tails = 1 space.
Look. Ask and answer.

107

Feeling Fit

In this unit, I will …
• name parts of the body.
• talk about the past.
• talk about good and bad habits.

Tick T for *True* or F for *False*.

1. He is rock-climbing.   T   F

2. The rocks are small.   T   F

3. He is wearing gloves.   T   F

Climbing the tsingy in Madagascar. Tsingy means 'Where you cannot walk barefoot'.

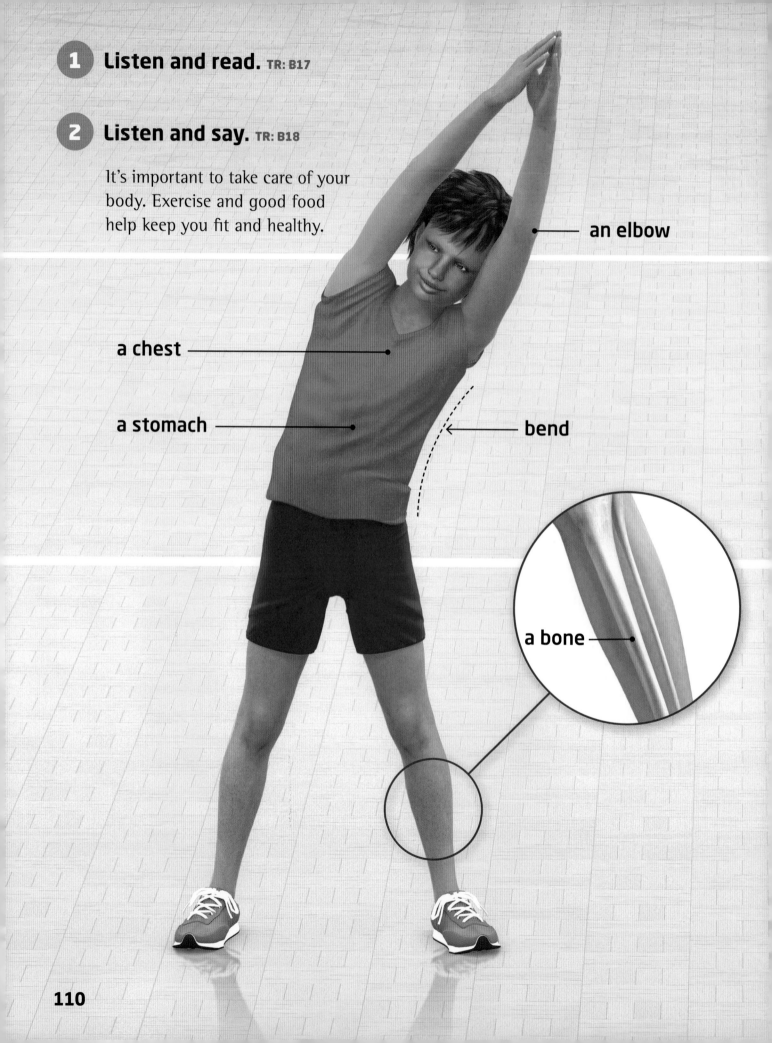

1 **Listen and read.** TR: B17

2 **Listen and say.** TR: B18

It's important to take care of your body. Exercise and good food help keep you fit and healthy.

an elbow

a chest

a stomach

bend

a bone

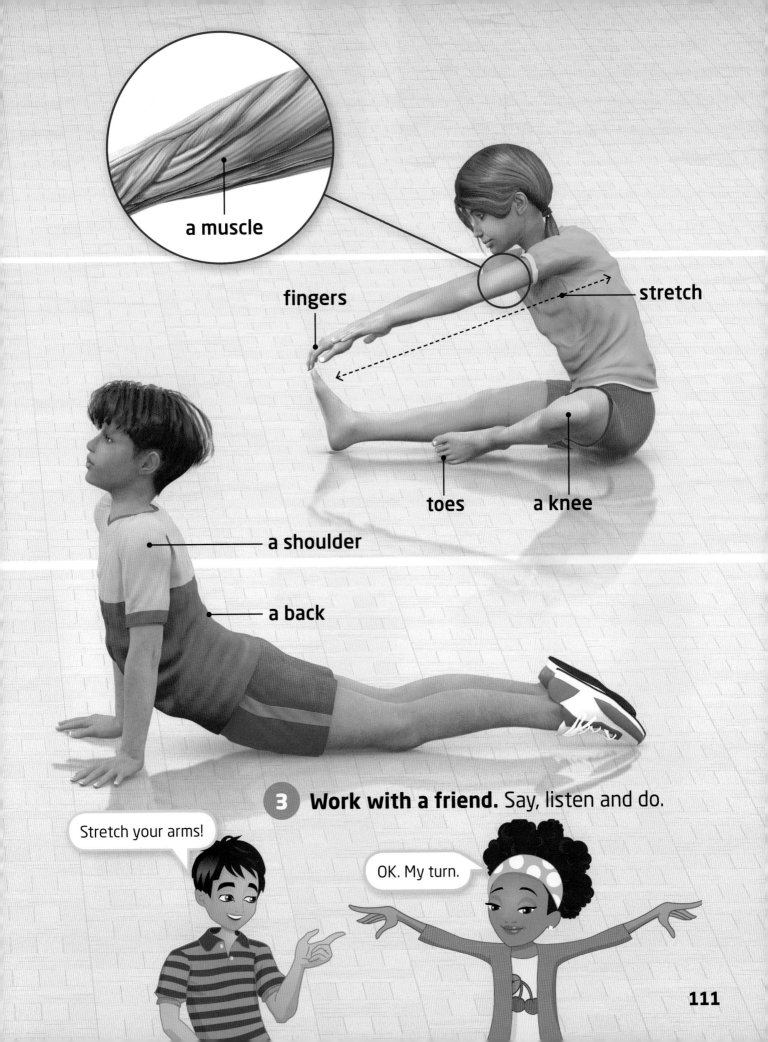

a muscle

fingers

stretch

toes

a knee

a shoulder

a back

3 **Work with a friend.** Say, listen and do.

Stretch your arms!

OK. My turn.

Let's Move

We like feeling fit.
We like having fun.
We like playing a lot.
Let's move now, everyone!

We want to feel healthy.
We want to get fit.
Come on, everybody.
Stand up, don't sit!

What did you do
            to get fit yesterday?
What did you do to feel strong?
What did you do
            to feel happy yesterday?
What did you do?

Did you move your legs? Yes, I did!
Did you stretch your back? I did that a lot!
Did you get enough sleep last night?
                            Yes, I did!
Did you have a healthy snack?
                        Oh no, I forgot!

Don't worry. Tomorrow is another day.
You can try again. It's OK!

We like feeling fit.
We like having fun.
We like playing a lot.
Let's jump now, everyone!

CHORUS

What did you do to get fit yesterday?
What did you do to feel strong?
What did you do to feel happy yesterday?
What did you do?

Did you stretch your muscles? Yes, I did!
Did you touch your toes? I did that a lot!
Did you bend your knees? Yes, I did!
Did you wiggle your nose? Oh no, I forgot!

Don't worry. Tomorrow is another day.
You can try again. It's OK!

We like feeling fit.
We like having fun.
We like playing a lot.
Let's dance now, everyone!

CHORUS

5 **Work in a group.** Act out an activity
for your group to guess. Take turns.

Did you **wash** your hands this morning?   Yes, I **did**.
Did you **brush** your teeth?   No, I **didn't**.
Did he **have** a shower?   Yes, he **did**.

6 **Read and look.** Write answers.

1. Did she have a shower yesterday? _____ No, she didn't. _____

2. Did she brush her teeth? _____

3. Did she eat fruit? _____

4. Did she go for a walk? _____

5. Did she ride her bike? _____

6. Did she make her bed? _____

7 **What about you?** Ask and answer. Write.

1. _____Did you ride_____ your bike yesterday? _____No, I didn't._____

2. _____ your teeth yesterday? _____

3. _____ a snack yesterday? _____

4. _____ a shower yesterday? _____

5. _____ football yesterday? _____

6. _____ your hands yesterday? _____

7. _____ TV yesterday? _____

8. _____ your homework yesterday? _____

8 **Work in a group.** Ask and answer questions.
Use these words.

| do your homework | eat salad | go for a walk |
| make your bed | play basketball | swim |

Did you go for a walk yesterday?

Yes, I did.

115

9 **Listen and say.** Read and write. TR: B21

do exercise

eat junk food

eat vegetables

get some rest

eat fruit

1. I ___eat fruit___ every day. I like apples, mangoes and grapes!

2. I _____ every day. I play football and go swimming.

3. I _____ every day. I love carrots, beans and potatoes.

4. I _____ every day. I relax after school and I sleep at night!

5. I _____ sometimes. I eat crisps and drink fizzy drinks.

10 **Stick in order (1 = most important).** Work with a friend.
Talk about what you think is important.

> My number one is exercise. It's very important to do exercise.

> My number one is fruit. I think it's important to eat fruit.

1   2   3   4   5

It's important to get **enough** sleep. Don't stay up **too** late.
I drink **enough** water. I don't eat **too** much junk food.

11 **Read and make true sentences about you.**
Underline the words.

1. I **drink** / **don't drink** too many fizzy drinks.

2. I **do** / **don't do** enough exercise.

3. I **drink** / **don't drink** enough water.

4. I **eat** / **don't eat** too many crisps.

5. I **watch** / **don't watch** too much TV.

6. I **get** / **don't get** enough sleep.

12 **Play a game.** Cut out the cards
on page 171. Choose a card, and
toss a coin. Play with a friend.

 Heads = good for you   **Tails =** bad for you

Tails. I watch too much TV. No points for me! Your turn.

Heads. I get enough sleep. One point for me!

Are You Playing Enough Computer Games?

Do you get enough rest? Do you do enough exercise? It's important to get some rest *and* do some exercise every day. This gives you energy and keeps your muscles strong.

Many people play computer games. In some computer games, you only have to press buttons with your fingers. You can sit on the sofa and play. In other games, you need to move your whole body. It is fun because it is exercise and computer games together!

In some of these games, you hold a remote control in your hand. You swing it like a tennis racket or move it fast to run.

In some computer games, you don't need to touch anything! But how do these games work? The game console has a camera. This camera records your body and the way you move. It can see when you move your shoulders, your elbows, your knees, your whole body. You can pretend to throw a basketball and see yourself on the screen!

There are many dance games, too – dancing is a great way to keep fit. You just follow the moves on the screen and dance with the music!

remote control

screen

game console

You can control some computer games with your brain!

Weird but true

14 Read and circle.

1. It's important to get some rest and **dance** / **exercise** every day.

2. In some games, you hold a **remote control** / **game console** in your hand.

3. Exercise keeps your muscles **small** / **strong**.

4. In some computer games, the game console has a **camera** / **mobile phone**.

5. Dancing is a great way to **get rest** / **keep fit**.

15 Look and write.

In some computer games,

In other computer games,

16 Work with a friend. Talk about exercise with computer games. Do you think it's fun? Do you want to do it?

It's fun. You can play many different sports.

Yes. I've got a tennis computer game.

17 **Read.** Read about Daniel's favourite way to keep fit. He uses *because* to explain why he likes swimming.

Swim to keep fit!

Swimming is my favourite way to keep fit. It's great exercise and a lot of fun, too! I like it because you move all of your body. You use your arms, your shoulders, your legs – and all your muscles. Another reason I like it is because you can swim inside or outside. In winter, I go to the swimming pool. In summer, I sometimes swim in the sea and watch fish under the water. I like swimming in races, too. But my favourite thing to do is to splash water and have fun with my friends!

18 **Write.** How do you keep fit? What exercise or sport do you like? Why?

19 **Work in groups of three.** Read your writing to your group. Listen. Take turns. Complete the table.

Name	Activity	Why?

Our World

Be good to your body.

20 **Look and read.**

Take care of your body. Exercise.

Polar bear swimming under the Arctic ice.

21 **Read.** Talk and write.
How can you be good to your body?

I can exercise every day.

22 **Make a poster.** Work in a group. Make a Good Habits poster.

Make four sections on your paper.

Write the headings: *Keep fit, Stay clean, Eat good food, Keep safe.*

Write sentences and draw or cut out pictures.

Sign your name.

We think it's important to sleep for eight hours every night.

Good Habits

Keep fit

Sleep eight hours every night.

Do some exercise every day.

Stay Clean

Wash your hands before meals.

Brush your teeth every morning and night.

Eat good food

Eat lots of fruit and vegetables.

Have healthy snacks.

Keep safe

On your bike, wear clothes to protect you.

Be careful when you walk outside.

Mi Young   Jae Sun

Let's Celebrate!

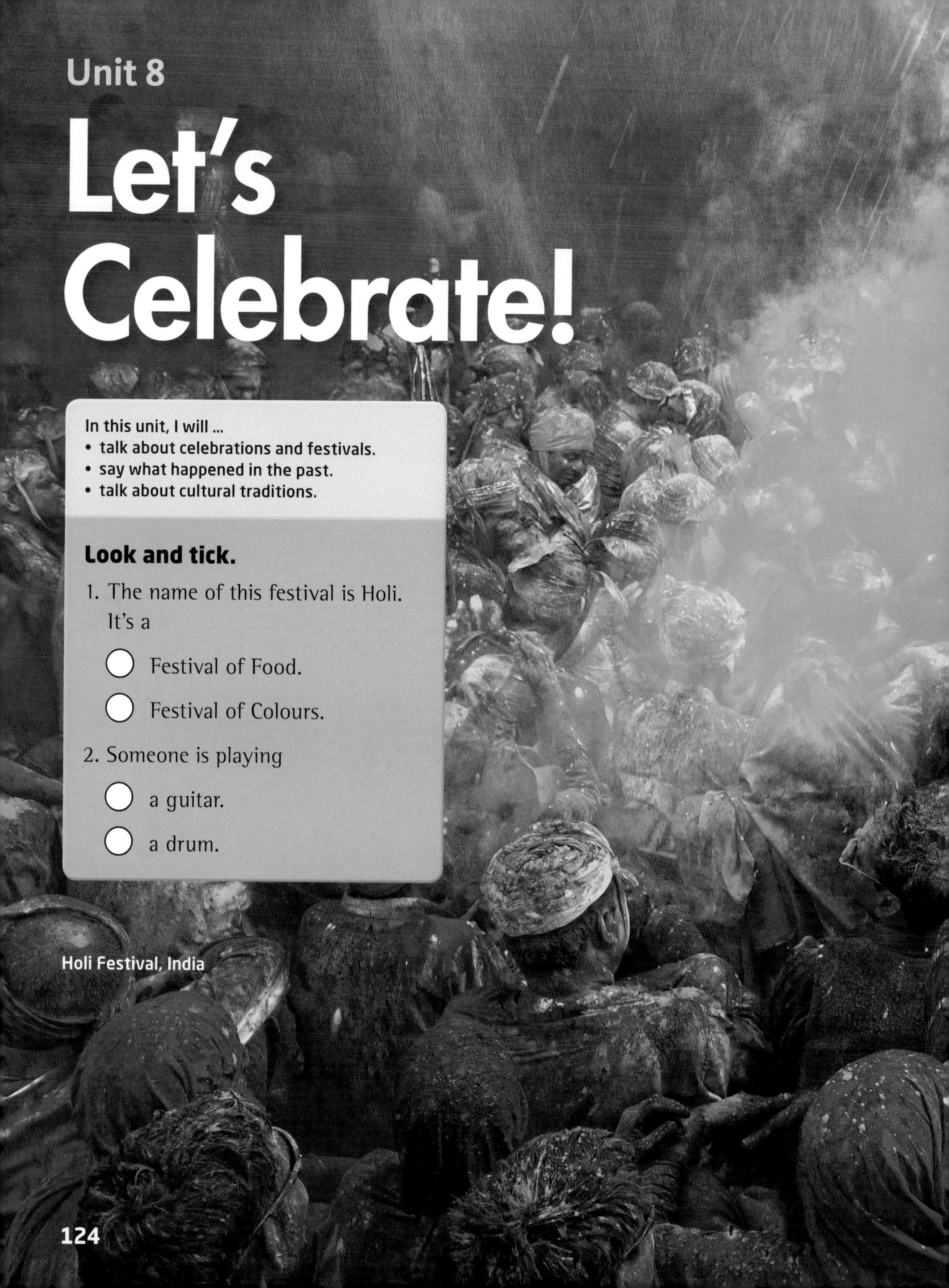

In this unit, I will …
- talk about celebrations and festivals.
- say what happened in the past.
- talk about cultural traditions.

Look and tick.

1. The name of this festival is Holi.
   It's a

   ○ Festival of Food.

   ○ Festival of Colours.

2. Someone is playing

   ○ a guitar.

   ○ a drum.

Holi Festival, India

People all over the world have special celebrations.
They take time to remember the past, meet family
and friends, eat food and have fun!

a costume

a feast

a mask

a lantern

a party

fireworks

celebrate

remember

dance

dress up

decorations

a parade

3 **Work with a friend.** Ask and answer.

Do you like dressing up?

Yes, I do. I've got lots of costumes.

4 **Listen.** Read and sing. TR: B26

Celebrate!

We went to a carnival.
Everyone was there!
We dressed up, sang some songs
and watched a parade.

But best of all ...
We danced to music,
wonderful music.
We danced to music
all day long.

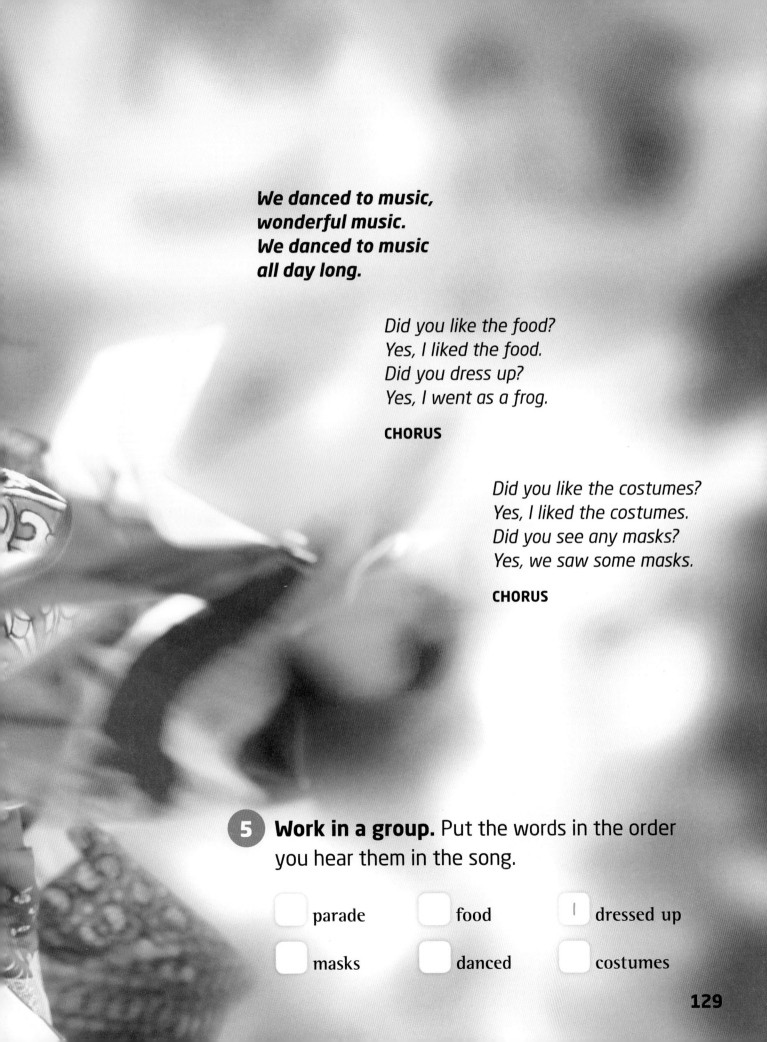

We danced to music,
wonderful music.
We danced to music
all day long.

Did you like the food?
Yes, I liked the food.
Did you dress up?
Yes, I went as a frog.

CHORUS

Did you like the costumes?
Yes, I liked the costumes.
Did you see any masks?
Yes, we saw some masks.

CHORUS

5 **Work in a group.** Put the words in the order you hear them in the song.

☐ parade   ☐ food   ☐ dressed up

☐ masks   ☐ danced   ☐ costumes

Did you **watch** the parade?   Yes, I **watched** the parade.
Did you **dance** at the party?   Yes, I **danced** at the party.

6 **Read and write.** Complete the sentences. Use these words.

dress up	like	listen	play	watch

Yesterday ...

1. I ___dressed up___ in my favourite costume. I was a superhero!

2. The parade was great. We _____ to music from many countries.

3. I _____ the food and the dancing. It was fun!

4. After dinner, all the children _____ games.

5. At night, we _____ the fireworks. They were incredible!

7 **What about you?** Think of a celebration. Write true sentences. Use these words.

celebrate	dance	like	listen	play	watch

1. <u>We celebrated my birthday.</u>

2. _____

3. _____

4. _____

5. _____

6. _____

8 **Work with a friend.** Ask questions about your celebration.

Did you play games at the party?

Yes, we played games. It was fun.

9 **Listen and say.** Read and write. TR: B28

a present

a birthday cake

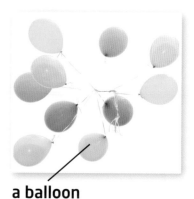

a candle

Come to my party!
What: My party!
When: 17th October
Where: My house

an invitation

a balloon

1. You write this on paper. You give it to your friends. _an invitation_

2. It tastes sweet. It usually has candles on top. _____

3. They are usually round. They have air inside. _____

4. They are long and thin. You put them on a birthday cake. _____

5. You use colourful paper to wrap it. You give it to people on

   their birthdays. _____

10 **Listen and stick.** TR: B29

1   2   3   4   5

Did you **go** to the parade yesterday?   Yes, I **went** to the parade.
Did you **see** the fireworks?   Yes, I **saw** the fireworks.
Did you **eat** cake at the party?   Yes, I **ate** a piece of cake at the party.

11 **These verbs change when you talk about the past.**
Match. Draw lines.

sing	wrote
drink	gave
wear	had
have	took
write	sang
give	went
take	drank
go	wore

12 **Play a game.** Cut out the cards on page 173. Play with a friend. Match and say sentences.

See. Saw. I saw lots of lanterns. Your turn.

No match for me. Your turn again.

see

saw

have

drank

November Celebrations

The Day of the Dead is a big festival in Mexico. People celebrate it on the first day of November. They remember and celebrate the dead people in their family. They sometimes decorate the graves in the cemetery with skeletons in special costumes. Families take a big feast to the cemetery, and they light candles and play music. Sometimes there are fireworks, too. People give sweets and chocolate in the shape of skulls. For Mexicans, skulls and skeletons are not scary and the festival is not sad. The Day of the Dead is a time for fun and happy celebrations.

Day of the Dead

In Thailand, the festival of Yi Peng usually happens in November, too. On the first day, there is a parade and people wear beautiful costumes. People make lanterns out of rice paper. They light small candles inside them. The warm air makes the lanterns go up into the sky. On the night of the festival, there are thousands of bright lanterns in the sky. It's very beautiful. People imagine that the lanterns are taking away the bad things in their lives. People also decorate their homes and gardens with paper lanterns. And on the last day, there are fireworks.

Festival of Yi Peng

In 2002, a sweet manufacturer made chocolate fireworks! 60 kilograms (132 pounds) of chocolate went up into the sky!

134

14 **Read.** Tick **T** for *True* or **F** for *False*.

1. The Day of the Dead is a sad festival in Mexico.   T (F)

2. On the Day of the Dead, families have food at the cemeteries.   T   F

3. At Yi Peng, there is a parade and there are fireworks.   T   F

4. There is only one lantern in the sky at the Yi Peng festival.   T   F

5. Both the Day of the Dead and the festival of Yi Peng are usually celebrated in November.   T   F

15 **Read.** Complete the table.

	Day of the Dead	Yi Peng
When is it?		
Why do they celebrate it?		
What do people do?		

16 **Work with a friend.** Look at the photographs. What can you see? What do you like?

I like the lanterns. I think they are beautiful.

I like the lanterns, too! And can you see those skulls?

135

17 **Read about Hiro and his favourite festival.** What title does Hiro use for his writing? The title tells you what you are reading about. It is short and simple. In the body text, Hiro uses words that describe what he saw, heard and did.

The Sapporo Snow Festival
by Hiro

Every year we have a snow festival. It is in February, in the winter. This year it was fantastic! It was very cold. I wore a snowsuit, boots, gloves and a hat. There was a lot to do, and we had so much fun. I went to see the beautiful snow sculptures with my brother and sister. My favourite sculpture was of two big dinosaurs. They looked scary! We played on the snow slides and in a snow maze, too! In the evening, we saw colourful lights, we listened to music, we ate hot dumplings and we drank hot chocolate to get warm! The festival was wonderful this year!

18 **Write.** Write about a celebration or festival. Think about what you wore, what you saw and what you did.

19 **Work in groups of three.** Read your writing to your group. Listen. Take turns. Complete the table.

Name	Celebration or festival	What did people see and do?

Our World

Celebrate your culture.

20 **Look and read.**

Enjoy your traditions
and festivals.

Elephant Festival, Jaipur, Rajasthan, India

21 **Read.** Talk and write.
How do you celebrate your culture?

Every year there is a parade in my town.

22 Make a parade mask.

Decorate it and describe it to the class.

Choose a celebration.

Do research.

Collect materials.

Decorate
your mask.

Now I can ...

○ talk about celebrations and festivals.

○ say what happened in the past.

○ talk about cultural traditions.

I made the eyes with white, blue and yellow paper.

Unit 9
My Weekend

In this unit, I will ...
- talk about spare time activities.
- talk about the past.
- talk about hobbies.

Look and tick.

The boy is

- ○ playing basketball.
- ○ playing volleyball.
- ○ playing football.

He is

- ○ tired.
- ○ happy.
- ○ bored.

Tegucigalpa, Honduras

1 **Listen and read.** TR: B32

2 **Listen and say.** TR: B33

The weekend is a time to relax and do fun things. Sometimes we stay at home. Other times we go out and visit places, play outside or see friends.

eat out

go to the cinema

visit a museum

go on a picnic

stay at home

142

lose

win

exciting

interesting

text my friends

busy

go to the beach

3 **Work with a friend.**
Ask and answer.

What do you do at the weekend?

Sometimes I go to the cinema. What about you?

Spare Time

Spare time! Spare time! Spare time is great!
There is no school and I can get up late.
In my spare time I like having fun.
I throw and catch! I jump and run!

What did you do at the weekend?
Did you stay at home? Did you have some fun?
What did you do at the weekend?
Did you go outside and play in the sun?

Did you go fishing?
Did you play tennis?
Did you go hiking?
What did you do?

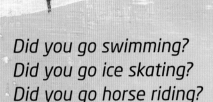

Did you go swimming?
Did you go ice skating?
Did you go horse riding?

I didn't go fishing or hiking.
I didn't go swimming or ice skating.
I played a game with my little brother.
I went to the cinema with
my mother.

CHORUS

Did you go fishing?
Did you play tennis?
Did you go hiking?
What did you do?

Did you go swimming?
Did you go ice skating?
Did you go horse riding?

I stayed at home.
I played with everyone!
I lost at tennis, but it was fun.
I texted friends. I helped cook dinner!
When I help out, I feel like a winner!

CHORUS

Spare time! Spare time! Spare time is great!
There is no school and I can get up late.
In my spare time I like having fun.
I dance and sing! I play and run!

5 **Work with a friend.** Talk.

1. What three things from the song
   do you do in your spare time?

2. What three things from the song
   don't you do in your spare time?

How was your weekend?   It was boring. I **didn't do** anything special.
What did you do?   I went to a football match.
Did your team win?   No, they **didn't win**. They lost.

6   **Read and write.** Complete the sentences.
Use these words.

went	didn't go	won	didn't win	didn't eat out	didn't watch

What did you do at the weekend?

1. We ___didn't go___ on a picnic because it was raining!

2. We _____ to the cinema. We saw a great film.

3. We played basketball on Saturday. We _____.
   We lost!

4. On Sunday we had lunch at home. We _____.

5. On Monday we didn't eat out. We _____ on a picnic.

6. Last weekend we _____ to the beach. The weather
   was bad.

7. Yesterday I _____ TV. I played computer games.

8. I went to the game. It was great! We _____!

7 **What about you?** Write about things you did and didn't do at the weekend.

Things I did

1. _____

2. _____

3. _____

4. _____

Things I didn't do

5. _____

6. _____

7. _____

8. _____

8 **Work with a friend.** Ask and answer.

How was your weekend?

It was boring!

Why?

I didn't go to the cinema. I didn't eat out. I stayed at home.

9 **Listen and say.** Read and write. TR: B36

go fishing

go hiking

go horse riding

go swimming

go ice skating

1. I _____go ice skating_____ in winter. I can go fast on the ice.

2. I _____ with my dad. We don't catch many fish!

3. I _____ sometimes. Horses can run very fast.

4. I _____ with my family. We go into the woods.

5. I _____ every weekend. I can swim very well now.

10 **Stick your favourite activities.** Work with a friend.
Ask and answer.

Do you want to go mountain climbing?

No, I don't. I want to go hiking.

1   2   3   4   5

148

What **do** you **do** at weekends?

What **did** you **do** last weekend?

We usually **go hiking**.

We **didn't go hiking**.

We **went swimming**.

11 **Look and write.**

What did Carlos do at the weekend?

1. _He went ice skating._ _____

2. _____

3. _____

4. _____

5. _____

12 **Play a game.** Cut out the game board on page 175.
Play with a friend. Take turns. Toss a coin.

What did you do last weekend?

Heads:
Yes + move
one space

Tails:
No

I didn't go shopping.

149

Wow! Look at That!

Museums are great places to visit at the weekend. They teach us about the world in fun ways. Many museums have special exhibitions for children. Other museums are ALL for children!

Are these dinosaurs escaping from a museum? At The Children's Museum in Indianapolis, USA, there are giant models of dinosaurs outside. Some of them are running away and others are looking in through the window!

Inside the museum there are real dinosaur fossils, rooms about science, art, culture, history and much more. You can learn about the stars in the planetarium, you can go to the theatre and you can even go rock climbing!

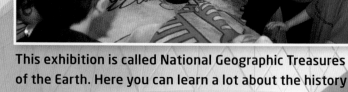

Weird but true

In Turkey, there is a museum of hair. It has hair from more than 16,000 people!

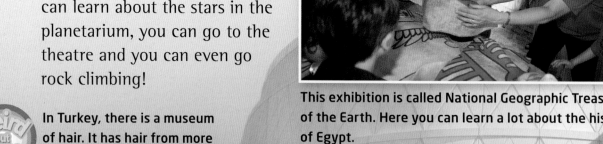

This exhibition is called National Geographic Treasures of the Earth. Here you can learn a lot about the history of Egypt.

This is a plan of part of the museum.
What is next to the trains?

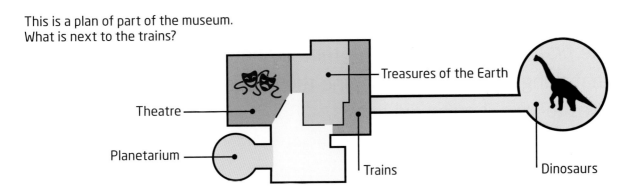

Theatre
Planetarium
Treasures of the Earth
Trains
Dinosaurs

14 **Read.** Match to make sentences.

1. The Children's Museum is

2. In the museum, there are trains

3. You can learn about the stars

4. There are giant models of dinosaurs

5. You can go to the theatre and you can

a. in the planetarium.

b. in Indianapolis, USA.

c. near the dinosaurs.

d. go rock climbing.

e. outside the museum.

15 **Read.** What's at the Children's Museum in Indianapolis?
Make a table. Write.

Things I know are there	Things I think are there
Giant models of dinosaurs	

16 **Work in groups of three.** Talk about museums you
know. Take turns. Ask and answer questions.

I went to a
toy museum.

What did you see?

17 **Read.** When you describe an event, you can use words like *first, then, next* and *after that* to show the order that things happened. Underline the words that Hassan uses to say when he did things.

My perfect weekend

I got up early on Saturday and it was warm and sunny. First, I had my favourite breakfast – a bowl of yoghurt, honey and nuts! After that, I went fishing with my friend Yildiray. We took lunch with us – we were out all day. In the evening, I watched TV with my brothers. On Sunday, we didn't get up early. I read my comic in bed. Then we got ready to see my favourite football team. We went to the stadium. My team won, of course! We sang and shouted a lot! It was a fantastic weekend!

18 **Write.** Describe a good weekend you had. What did you do?

19 **Work in a group.** Read your writing to your group. Listen. Take turns. Complete the table.

Name	What did he or she do?

NATIONAL GEOGRAPHIC

Our World

Try new things.

20 Look and read.

Discover the things
you love.

21 Read. Talk and write.
Write two things you would like to try.

I would like to go ice skating and skiing.

22 Make a class scrapbook.

Show and talk about your favourite activities. Present your work.

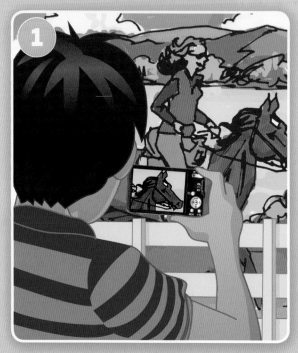

Take photos or draw pictures of five weekend activities you like.

Make a collage of your photos and drawings.

Write about your weekend activities.

Add your page to the class scrapbook.

Review

What Did You Do Yesterday?

Work with a friend. Use a coin. Heads = 2 spaces, Tails = 1 space.
Look. Ask and answer.

One to Ten!

Work with a friend. You have three minutes to answer the questions.

1. Write three parts of the body beginning with *e*.

2. When is your favourite festival?

3. Write two things you did at the weekend.

4. What are these?

5. What is this word? **v e e t e l a b g**

6.

> Do you do enough _____?
>
> Yes, I go running and I love swimming.

7. Write three things you do at a festival.

8. You've got fingers on your hands and _____

   on your feet.

9. Write three things you see at a birthday party.

10.

> What did you do at the weekend?

> I went _____!

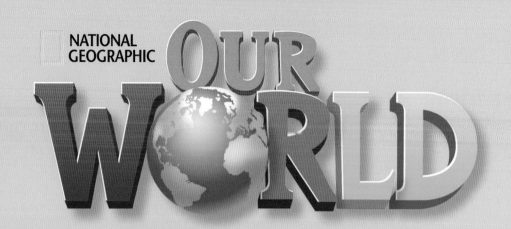

NATIONAL GEOGRAPHIC OUR WORLD

This is our world.
Everybody's got a song to sing.
Each boy and girl.
This is our world!

I say 'our', you say 'world'.
Our!
World!
Our!
World!

I say 'boy', you say 'girl'.
Boy!
Girl!
Boy!
Girl!

I say everybody move …
I say everybody stop …
Everybody stop!

This is our world.
Everybody's got a song to sing.
Each boy and girl.
This is our world!

1 **do my homework
in the evening**

the same?

2 **have lunch
at 12.00**

the same?

3 **wash my face
in the evening**

the same?

5 **have a snack
after school**

the same?

4 **brush my teeth
after breakfast**

the same?

6 **ride my bike
on Saturdays**

the same?

7 **watch TV**

the same?

8 **make my bed
in the morning**

the same?

never

never

sometimes

sometimes

usually

usually

always

always

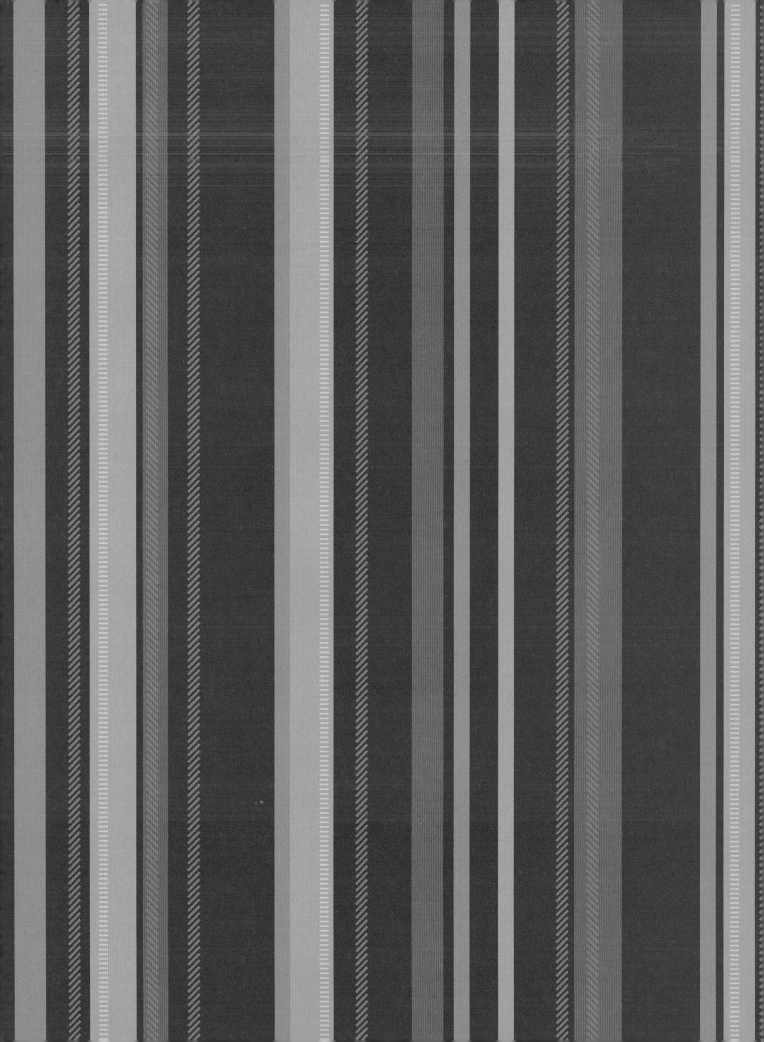

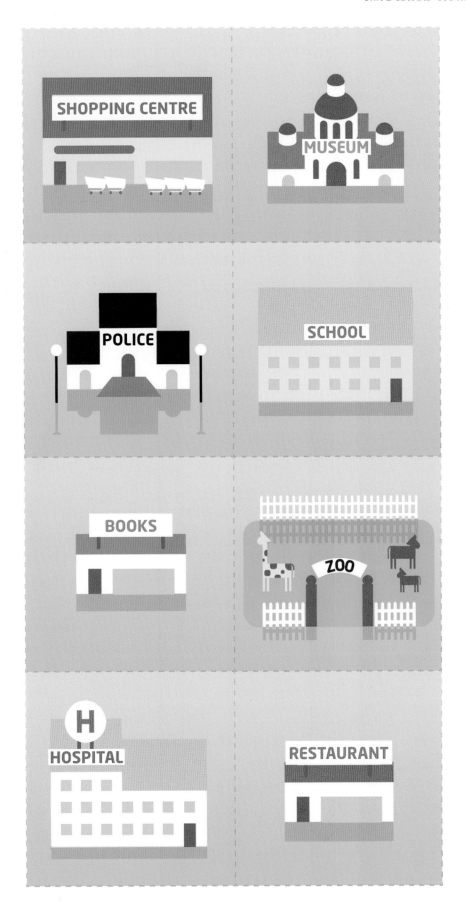

Jenny  **to school**	**Sam**  **to school**	**Jenny** **likes**  **for breakfast**
Sam **likes**  **for breakfast**	**Jenny** **wants to** 	**Sam** **wants to** 
Jenny  **at 9.00 p.m.**	**Sam**  **at 9.00 p.m.**	**Jenny**  **on Saturdays**
Sam  **on Saturdays**	**Jenny** **likes** 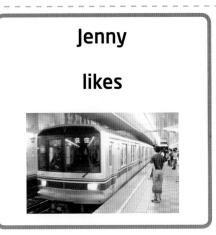	**Sam** **likes** 

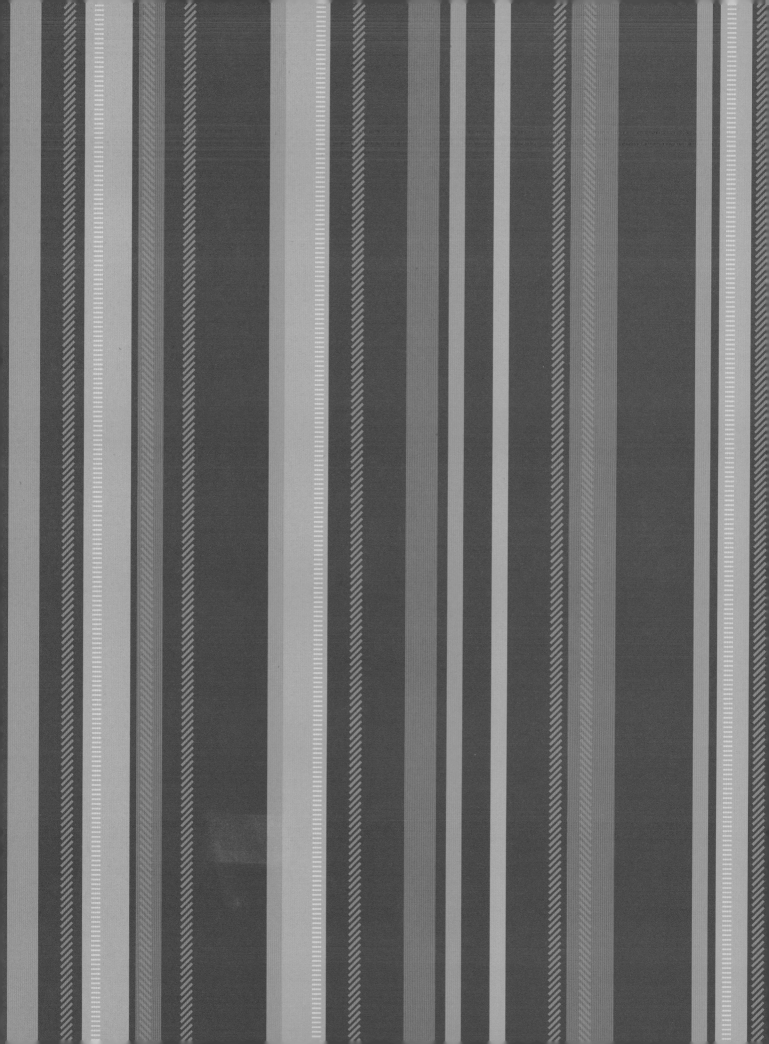

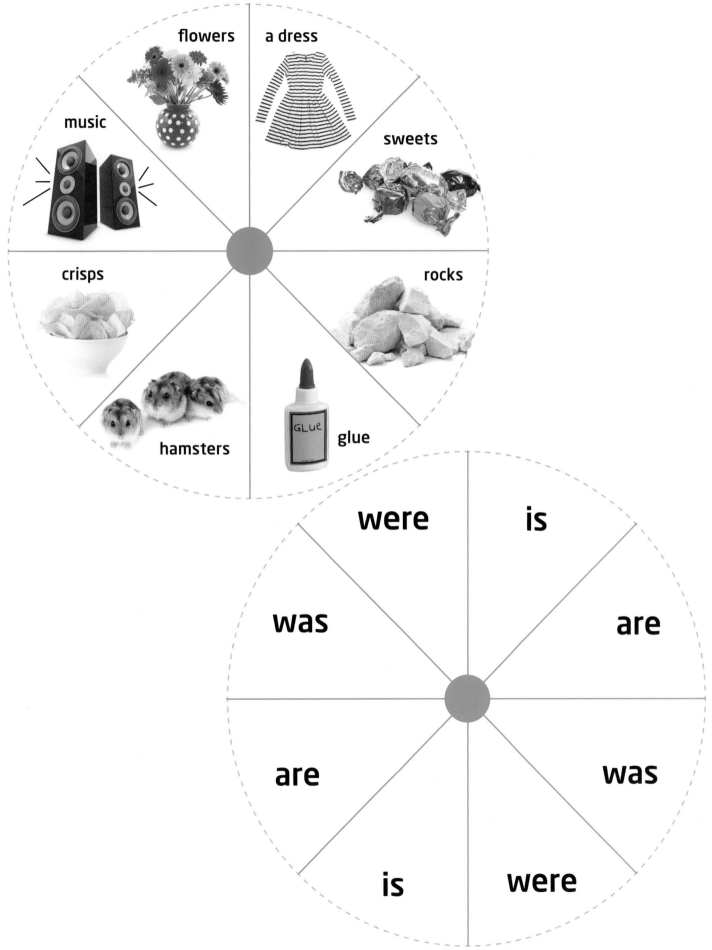

flowers

a dress

music

sweets

crisps

rocks

hamsters

glue

were

is

was

are

are

was

is

were

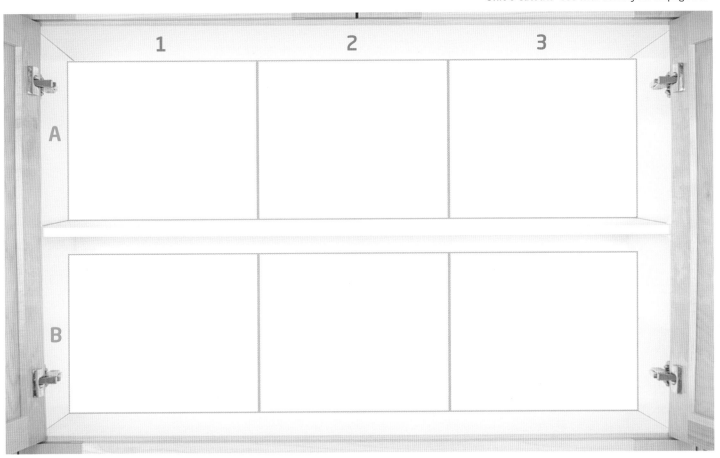

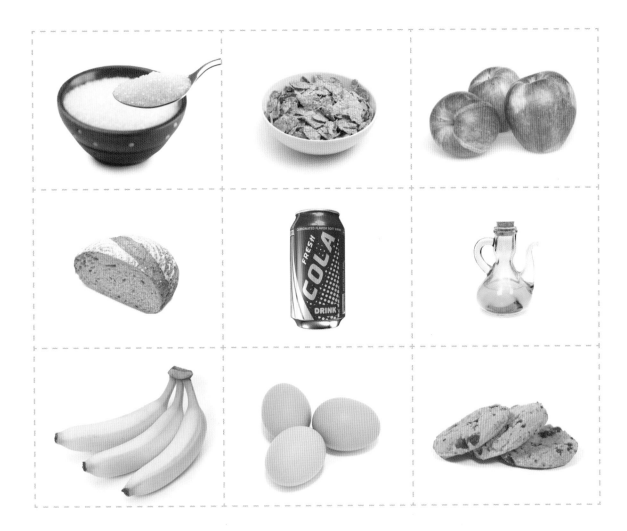

take

wear

took

wore

eat

drink

ate

drank

see

sing

saw

sang

go

have

went

had

Start

1

2

3

6

5

4

7

8

9

End

12

11

10

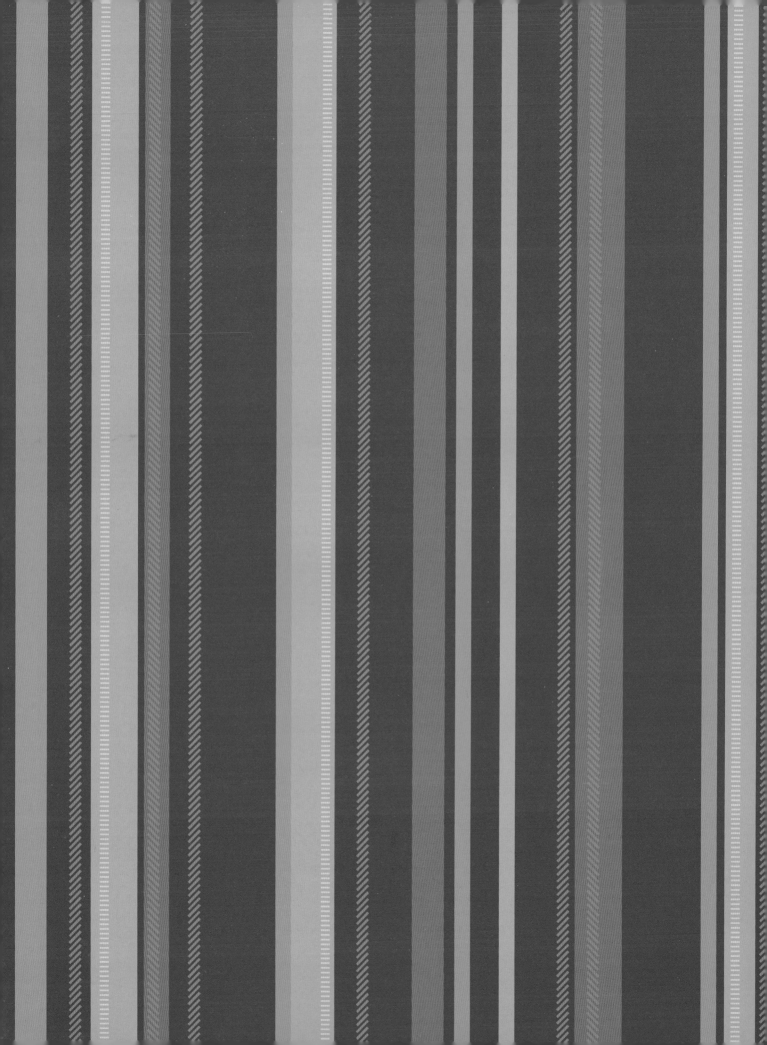